pucker

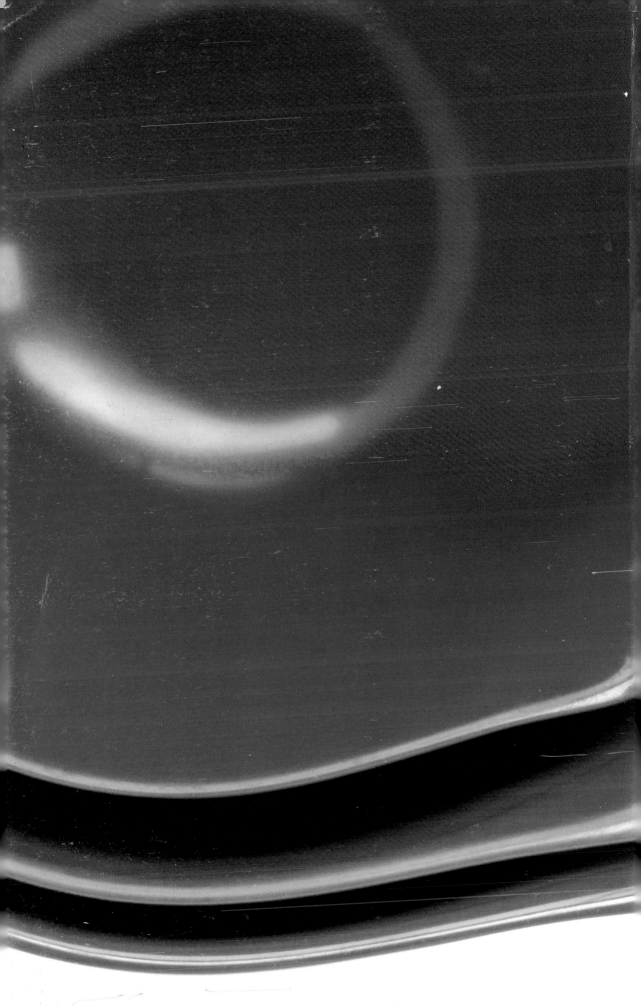

pucker

A Cookbook for Citrus Lovers

GWENDOLYN RICHARDS

whitecap

Whitecap Books is known for its expertise in the cookbook market, and has
produced some of the most innovative and familiar titles found in kitchens
across North America. Visit our website at www.whitecap.ca.

EDITOR: Jenny Govier
DESIGNER: Diane Robertson
FOOD PHOTOGRAPHER AND STYLIST: Gwendolyn Richards
PROOFREADER: Jeffrey Bryan

Printed in Canada

LIBRARY AND ARCHIVES CANADA CATALOGUING IN PUBLICATION

Richards, Gwendolyn, author
          Pucker : a cookbook for citrus lovers / Gwendolyn Richards.
Includes index.
ISBN 978-1-77050-227-7 (pbk.)
          1. Cooking (Citrus fruits). 2. Cookbooks. I. Title.
TX813.C5R53 2014   641.6′4304   C2014-903224-2

The publisher acknowledges the financial support of the Government of Canada
through the Canada Book Fund (CBF) and the Province of British Columbia
through the Book Publishing Tax Credit.

21 20 19 18 17 16 15 14   1 2 3 4 5 6 7 8

To my grandfather, who nurtured
in me a lifelong love of food.

To Michelle, who always thought starting
a food blog was an excellent idea.

And to Andrea, who never saw
lemons, only lemonade.

table of contents

foreword

by Anna Olson

WHAT A DELIGHT to see a worker-bee ingredient of the kitchen get its dues. In a way like the onion, the affordable, affable and easy-to-use citrus family often gets overlooked but just imagine what our dishes would be without that appropriate pucker. Our salads would be heavy and flat without the gentle acidity to balance them, our main dishes would lack that perfume of citrus zest and our sweet treats, well, they would be cloying and lack any dimension.

Someone who spends time exploring cooking and baking can also appreciate the science that citrus lends, and is apparent in this book. Ricotta cannot exist without that small measure of lemon juice, while the acidity of lime or lemon juice keeps eggs at that just-right consistency within curds and key lime pie, and savoury dishes are better for the addition of zest, aromatic oils and juice for that tartness.

Gwendolyn captures the magic of citrus in this book, and before you've flipped through half of its pages your mouth will be watering and you'll be trying to decide which recipe to make first. You can just smell the citrus in the air—get your zesters, peelers, reamers and juicers ready to . . .

. . . pucker up!

introduction

I ONCE REACHED OUT to a guy on an Internet dating site simply because in his write-up he noted he liked lemon-flavoured desserts—and despite the fact he was far out of my romantic (and geographic) league. In a brief moment of fantasy, I imagined us sharing pieces of lemon layer cake sandwiching a curd filling or cloud-like lemon soufflés. Our mutual love for slightly sour and sunny desserts was not enough to persuade him to respond.

That's okay.

In the end, I realized I'd really rather have the entire lemon dessert to myself anyway.

That citrus kiss, that tang, that pucker; it almost makes me swoon sometimes. I can easily pass up offers for chocolate cake, rich puddings, even cheesecake. But give me a dessert menu or put me in front of a bakery display case with something flavoured with citrus and I will zero in on it, fixate on it, unable to say no.

And I'm not alone. We lemon (and lime and grapefruit) lovers are abundant. Maybe not to the point where we outnumber those with chocolate addictions, but we hold our own. We are the ones who like a little more sour with our sweet, some tart sharpness, brightness, dishes with complexity. We like it in our desserts; we like it in our soups, salads and baked goods. We find few things are not elevated by a squeeze of citrus overtop.

Some may think my love goes too far. When I first started food writing on the side, as a way to combat the emotional roller coaster of covering crime and calamity for a daily news-paper, my editor had to put me on a lemon ban because all I kept pitching were stories featuring those fruits, full of bright acid and sunshine flavour: drinks with lemon, cookies with lime, lemon-spiked cakes and bars. (Though this, of course, did not stop me from continuing to pursue my love for the pucker on my own time; my blog is packed with recipes featuring lemon, lime and, more recently, grapefruit.)

Still, others understand. There's a reason the most popular post on my blog is for Chewy Lemon Cookies; it's also the recipe that garners the most search engine traffic on the site. When I bring my signature Lime Sugar Cookies into the newsroom, the rush to grab one is much faster than when I bring in many other goodies. (Although journalists will flock to pretty much any free food.)

In the heat of summer, acidic citrus is refresh-ing and light. In the doldrums of winter, it adds a freshness and dimension to overly rich and sometimes flabby-tasting dishes. It always pro-vides something a little special to dishes without breaking the bank. Forget truffle oil, fancy salts and expensive spices; for less than a dollar, a lemon or lime adds instant luxe.

Almost every cuisine in the world uses citrus. But there is a geographic division—for the most part—between which areas of the world tend toward limes and which fare is far more lemon heavy. Although originally believed to come from India, Burma and China, lemons seem more commonly associated with European dishes, especially from those countries ringing the Mediterranean. The tart yellow fruits were mostly used as ornaments in gardens until the 15th century, when they finally made their way into kitchens. Italy started the first major cultivation of the fruit in Genoa around that time.

Limes originated in Southeast Asia and were believed to have been introduced to India and the Middle East by Arab and Persian traders. It is thought that they, like lemons, were spread to the West Indies and, ultimately, North America by explorers, including Christopher Columbus. These smaller green citrus—which have more acid and sugar than their lemon counterparts—are more widely used in recipes from South Asia and India.

Many of the recipes in this book reflect this geographic citrus split. Fragrant and aromatic limes appear in dishes that have a Thai, Vietnamese or Indian flavour, while lemons are used more often in Italian- and French-inspired dishes.

Unlike lemons and limes, grapefruits—so named for the way they hang in clusters in trees—did not originate in Asia, but in the West Indies. This hybrid citrus, born of the combination of sweet orange and the giant pomelo, was first found in Barbados in the 1700s and later brought to Florida in the early 19th century. The United States today grows the most grapefruits in the world, almost three times as many as runner-up China.

Culinary cousins of a sort, these three types of citrus—lemons, limes and grapefruits—share a sour taste, in varying degrees, and are known for being high in vitamin C. In the 19th century, British sailors consumed lemons and limes as a preventive measure against scurvy, which led to the nickname "limey."

There are numerous varieties of citrus fruits, from the nubby-skinned kaffir lime to the strange and alien-looking Buddha's hand, which doesn't actually contain flesh, just incredibly aromatic skin and pith that isn't bitter. The finger lime is full of little bubbles of juicy flesh that have landed the fruit the nickname "lime caviar." Meyer lemons are a hybrid, believed to be a cross between a lemon and an orange. Their colour looks like a mix of the two and their skins are much thinner; there is almost no pith on a Meyer lemon.

I'm a fan of citrus in all its variations, but for the purpose of this book, I've stuck to the four most readily available: lemons, Meyer lemons—which can usually be found in the winter months in many grocery stores—limes and grapefruits. For most of my recipe testing, I used ruby red grapefruits because I like them straight up—cut in half, segmented and sprinkled with a bit of sugar—when I'm not using them for other dishes. I also like the soft pink colour against the green avocados in my salad and the way the segments pop when mixed with a creamy risotto, though any type of grapefruit will work.

The saying goes that when life hands you lemons, you should make lemonade.

I'm all for making the best of a bad situation, but I would never think being gifted lemons is a bad thing. Even after consuming several hundred lemons, limes and grapefruits in the last year while researching and perfecting recipes for this cookbook, I'm still as much in love with them as ever.

I will always crave that pucker.

tools, tips, tricks and techniques

Basic tools are all you need to get the most out of a citrus fruit. Time and again, I reach for three while cooking and baking: a microplane zester, a wooden reamer and a fine-mesh sieve.

Flavour comes from the juice of the coloured flesh inside the fruits, but a lot can also be found in the rind. Zesting just the coloured part of the citrus rind and adding it to recipes adds a huge boost of flavour that the juice of these fruits just can't impart. The trick, though, is to only get the zest and not the bitter white pith that lies between it and the flesh. A microplane zester, with its sharp, shallow teeth, rarely cuts into that bitter layer. One of mine is actually a true woodworking rasp, but numerous brands manufacture microplane zesters specifically for citrus fruits.

For longer pieces of the rind, I use a vegetable peeler to skin only the outer part of the citrus fruit. If I have taken off too much of the bitter pith with the peel, I lay out the piece, skin side down, and use a sharp paring knife to carefully slice away any of the white part.

Many of my recipes call for both zest and juice. Always zest first and then squeeze. But, in recipes in which the fruit is zested at the very end for a final touch, don't do that part in advance. Citrus zest can dry out quickly and lose some of its bright flavour, so it's best to wait.

Wash the citrus before zesting to get anything off the skin that would otherwise end up in the dish. Once they have been zested, citrus fruits harden and become nearly unusable. They will last a day or so if wrapped in plastic and stored in the fridge, but it's best to juice them immediately after taking off the rind. Once squeezed, citrus juice will last several days in a covered container in the fridge, but can also be frozen in ice cube trays and used later. Simply thaw and proceed with recipes as normal.

Lemons have a longer shelf life than limes and can sit on the counter for about a week or so. At that point, it's best to store them in the fridge, where they will keep for a few weeks before they start to wrinkle. Limes, on the other hand, should be refrigerated after a day or two as they will harden much more quickly, making them nearly impossible to cut and squeeze. Grapefruits stay fresh for about as long as lemons.

A wooden reamer is a simple and effective way to get juice out of citrus. Squeezing the fruit as you bore into it with the reamer helps extract as much of the juice as possible. Plastic versions also work, but I find they aren't as efficient. (Juicers made from plastic, glass or pottery that are essentially reamers surrounded by a bowl to collect the juice are great, but harder to find than wooden reamers.)

Finally, a fine-mesh sieve is the best way to remove seeds, seed fragments and pulp. For most of my recipes, unless otherwise noted, I've only removed seeds and seed fragments but not the pulp, which does not usually affect the final dish. When using a sieve, though, I use the back of a spoon to push the bits of pulp against the mesh to extract as much juice as possible.

When I make a large batch of cocktails or recipes that call for a lot of juice, I occasionally pull out an inexpensive juicer I picked up several years ago. While handy for large projects, it's hardly necessary. But it does save a lot of time when staring down a huge pile of lemons that all need to be squeezed.

Any lemon will give off about three or four tablespoons of juice, while limes can produce about three. To get the most from the fruit, roll it on a counter or hard surface, pressing down with your palm to give it a sort of internal squeeze, which will release a bit more juice.

A warm citrus fruit will impart more juice, but a cold one is easier to peel and zest.

When it comes to buying citrus, look for lemons, limes and grapefruits that are firm, heavy for their size, and smooth, and that have colourful, unblemished skins. Those with nubby, pebbly skin tend to have more pith and less flesh, so they yield less juice. Give them a good smell; if there is a lot of fragrance, they will usually yield quality juice and zest.

help, i've got leftovers

So, a recipe calls for citrus juice, but not all of what you managed to squeeze out. I love leftovers, but I hate waste. I tried hard to use the zest and juice of entire citrus fruits in my recipes so there was nothing left at the end, but it's not always possible. Here are a few ways to use up those last bits of lemon or lime juice:

- Store in a covered container in the fridge for a couple of days to use in other recipes that don't require zest.

- Use in a cocktail like the Whisky Sour or Paloma (page 9 and 22).

- Freeze leftovers in an ice cube tray for use later. You'll be able to fit about 1 tablespoon per cube in the tray, making it easy to measure later. Once frozen, pop them out of the tray and store in a freezer bag. You can also freeze the zest or peels for later use, so, when in doubt, zest the citrus first and save it for later.

- Add to still or sparkling water for a refreshing drink. Lemon and lime are also really great in cola.

- Combine with a bit of sugar or honey in a cup of tea.

- Add to salad dressings—instead of, or as a supplement to, vinegar—for a citrus twist.

ten other ways to use a lemon

Not just tasty, lemons are a multi-purpose fruit.

They're good for dispersing bad odours and cleaning pots, pans and cutting boards. When mixed with a few other ingredients, they are an effective sore throat remedy. Even after almost all the juice has been squeezed out, you can still wring a bit more use out of these fruits.

1. Freshen a cutting board—especially one used for slicing and dicing onions and garlic—by halving a lemon, squeezing its juice over the board and sprinkling the board with coarse salt. Use the squeezed half to rub in the salt, scouring all over. Rinse and then repeat on the other side with the other half.

2. Use cut lemons to remove pungent fish, onion and garlic smells from your hands.

3. Deodorize a garbage disposal by blitzing a squeezed or unsqueezed lemon in it with some warm water running.

4. Get rid of soap residue and hard water stains in the bathroom by scrubbing with a cut lemon.

5. Revive tarnished brass, copper and stainless steel, as well as aluminum pots and pans, to their former shiny glory with a little lemon. For aluminum pots, rub a halved lemon all over and then rinse and dry. Coat copper and other metal pots with a paste of lemon juice and salt and leave for a few minutes. Wash them in water, rinse thoroughly and then dry.

6. Clean out the microwave by combining the juice of a lemon with a cup of water in a bowl and cooking it on high for about five minutes. The steam from the lemon-and-water mixture will loosen any hardened food. Once the time is up, use a clean cloth to wipe down the microwave walls.

7. Lighten hair with lemon juice, just as with the once-popular Sun-In spray. Mix ¼ cup (60 mL) of lemon juice with ¾ cup (185 mL) of water and rinse your hair with it. Sit out in the sun until your hair is dry.

8. Remove dead skin and work on blackheads using the natural acid in citrus, which acts as a gentle exfoliant. Take a slice of lemon and gently scrub it over your face for a few minutes and then rinse with cold water.

9. Make an air freshener and add some humidity—especially useful during dry prairie winters—by boiling some water with slices of a whole lemon in it. Even cut-up pieces of rind are enough.

10. Lemons can soothe sore throats. This is my favourite remedy: Combine the juice from a large wedge of lemon, a splash of hot water and honey to taste. (Add a shot of whisky or bourbon to really knock that cold out.)

a few additional notes

- There is no substitute for fresh citrus juice, so please avoid those bottles of shelf-stable lemon or lime juice in the grocery store.

- Unless otherwise specified, I use salted butter in my recipes. Unsalted butter does give more control over the salt content in dishes, but I'd rather just buy one type, and the salted stuff is better on toast. If you prefer using unsalted butter, you'll want to compensate by adding a little more salt, roughly half a teaspoon for every cup of butter called for in a recipe.

- Eggs are standard large. For baking, let them come to room temperature before adding.

- Flour is all-purpose.

- Although I use a stand mixer for many of my baking recipes, hand-held beaters will work just as well. For years I had neither and simply beat everything by hand, which, while more time consuming, is also fine. Use whatever you have on hand. The key is to achieve the same end result (pale and fluffy butter and sugar, as an example), so just watch for that to happen instead of paying close attention to the time suggestions.

- In baking, you may be tempted to throw in that last teaspoon of juice from the citrus you squeezed. Resist! The interaction between leaveners and the acid is carefully calibrated, and that little bit extra can be enough to throw things off, leading cookies to spread too thin or cakes to rise wonkily and then fall. (For main dishes, soups and salads, this won't be a problem.)

drinks

appetizers

drinks &
appetizers

whisky sour

1½ ounces (45 mL) whisky or
  bourbon
1 ounce (30 mL) lemon juice
½ to ¾ ounces (15 to 22.5 mL)
  Simple Syrup (see below)

The first whisky sour I ever ordered was in the lounge at the Hotel Vancouver after my university friend Julie, who had been living in Ireland, insisted I give it a try. I learned two lessons that night: the first, that I should always trust her when it comes to cocktail suggestions, and the second, that you can always trust a hotel bar to make a good whisky sour. This is my favourite version to make when I'm at home, though I often substitute bourbon these days.

Add a handful of ice to a cocktail shaker, then add the whisky and lemon juice and the Simple Syrup to taste. Shake until the vessel is cold in your hand and everything is well mixed, about 15 to 20 seconds. (Use a towel to protect your hands from the cold if that helps you shake for longer.) Strain into a rocks glass.

MAKES 1 COCKTAIL

simple syrup

Combine equal parts sugar and water in a small pot. Set over medium heat and stir occasionally until the sugar has just dissolved. Remove from heat and let cool. Will keep for a few weeks in a covered container in the fridge.

meyer lemon bourbon sour

1½ ounces (45 mL) bourbon
   or whisky
1 ounce (30 mL) Meyer lemon
   juice
½ ounce (15 mL) Simple Syrup
   (page 9)
1 egg white

The sweeter and more fragrant flavour of Meyer lemons makes for a great sour. This one uses the traditional egg white to make it frothy and light, but it can be omitted if you're not keen on raw eggs. Unlike other shaken cocktails, the egg white and other ingredients are combined first before the ice is added and then shaken again to chill everything; this makes the egg white light and frothy without diluting the cocktail.

Add the bourbon or whisky, Meyer lemon juice, Simple Syrup and egg white to a cocktail shaker and shake vigorously for about 10 seconds. Add a handful of ice and shake until the vessel is cold in your hand and everything is well mixed, about another 15 to 20 seconds. (Use a towel to protect your hands from the cold if that helps you shake for longer.) Strain into a rocks glass.

MAKES 1 COCKTAIL

sidecar

sugar to rim the glass
2 ounces (60 mL) cognac
1 ounce (30 mL) Cointreau
½ ounce (15 mL) lemon juice

It was the allure of freshly squeezed lemon juice that had me ordering my first sidecar and then, later, making them at home based on the Barefoot Contessa Ina Garten's recipe, found in one of her cookbooks. When it came time to add a recipe to my own cookbook, I did further research, trying a few different takes on this classic cocktail. I didn't like any of them, but when I poured them all into the same glass and took a sip, the result was a cocktail I loved. So, this is my accidental, and now favourite, version.

Sprinkle a few spoonfuls of sugar onto a plate. After squeezing a lemon for the juice, run the rind around the rim of a martini glass and then press the glass into the sugar. Set the glass aside while you mix the drink.

Add a handful of ice to a cocktail shaker, then add the cognac, Cointreau and lemon juice. Shake until the vessel is cold in your hand and everything is well mixed, about 15 to 20 seconds. (Use a towel to protect your hands from the cold if that helps you shake for longer.) Strain into a martini glass.

MAKES 1 COCKTAIL

lemon drop martini

sugar to rim the glass
2 ounces (60 mL) vodka
½ ounce (15 mL) lemon juice
½ ounce (15 mL) Simple Syrup
  (page 9)
lemon slices (optional)

The quintessential lemon cocktail, this martini is full of pucker.

Sprinkle a few spoonfuls of sugar onto a plate. After squeezing a lemon for the juice, run the rind around the rim of a martini glass and then press the glass into the sugar. Set the glass aside while you mix the drink.

Add a handful of ice to a cocktail shaker, then add the vodka, lemon juice and Simple Syrup. Shake until the vessel is cold in your hand and everything is well mixed, about 15 to 20 seconds. (Use a towel to protect your hands from the cold if that helps you shake for longer.) Strain into the prepared martini glass. Garnish with a slice of lemon, if desired.

MAKES 1 COCKTAIL

moscow mule

4 ounces (125 mL) cold ginger
  beer
2 ounces (60 mL) vodka
½ ounce (15 mL) lime juice
lime wedge

An icy drink of ginger and lime—with some kick from the
vodka—this is a nice summer cocktail. It's traditionally served in
a copper mug, but I promise not to tell if we all just want to use
regular glasses.

In a copper mug—if you have one —or a highball glass, mix the
ginger beer, vodka and lime juice, stirring lightly. Add ice and
garnish with a lime wedge.

MAKES 1 COCKTAIL

greyhound

4 ounces (125 mL) grapefruit
  juice
2 ounces (60 mL) vodka

My drink of choice in university was vodka and boxed pink grape-fruit juice. I didn't realize at the time it actually had a name. These days I use freshly squeezed juice, making this highball even better than I remember.

Add ice to a highball glass, then pour in the juice and vodka. Stir well.

MAKES 1 COCKTAIL

salty dog

coarse salt to rim the glass

4 ounces (125 mL) grapefruit
 juice

2 ounces (60 mL) gin

Essentially a greyhound, but with aromatic gin substituted for vodka, the salty dog also features a salt-rimmed glass, like a margarita.

Sprinkle a few spoonfuls of coarse salt onto a plate. Dip the edge of a Tom Collins or highball glass in water and press it into the salt. Fill the glass with ice cubes, then add the grapefruit juice and gin. Stir well.

MAKES 1 COCKTAIL

paloma

coarse salt to rim the glass

2 ounces (60 mL) tequila

2 ounces (60 mL) grapefruit
juice

½ ounce (15 mL) lime juice

½ ounce (15 mL) Simple Syrup
(page 9)

2 ounces (60 mL) sparkling
water

Tangy grapefruit and aromatic lime come together with tequila for this bright drink. A bit reminiscent of a margarita, especially with the salt rim, this is excellent for summer sipping.

Sprinkle a few spoonfuls of coarse salt onto a plate. After squeezing the lime for the juice, run the rind around the rim of a highball glass and press the glass into the salt. Combine the tequila, grapefruit juice, lime juice and Simple Syrup in the glass and mix thoroughly. Top with ice and then sparkling water.

MAKES 1 COCKTAIL

lemonade

1 cup (250 mL) lemon juice
1 cup (250 mL) Simple Syrup
  (page 9)
pinch salt (optional)
4 cups (1 L) cold water
lemon slices (optional)

The thought of lemonade evokes mental pictures of kids selling it out in front of their houses and people sitting out on the porch sipping from glasses sweating from the sweltering heat. It is the essential summer thirst quencher. (Though I am certainly not suggesting that's the only time we should drink it.) This is a classic recipe for a classic drink.

In a large pitcher, combine the lemon juice, Simple Syrup and salt (which adds a slight complexity, but is optional). Give it a good stir to combine and to dissolve the salt. Pour in the water and stir again, then add a couple of handfuls of ice. Top with lemon slices to garnish.

MAKES ABOUT 6 CUPS (1.5 L)

sean's lime soda

juice of 2 limes
2 tablespoons (30 mL) Simple
    Syrup (approximately)
    (page 9)
sparkling water

I was visiting home one summer when my stepdad, Sean, poked his head into the living room and asked if I wanted a lime soda. Using the juice of two limes, a heavy splash of hummingbird food (basically, watered-down simple syrup) and some sparkling water, he concocted a quick drink that was perfectly refreshing. Since I never have hummingbird food in my fridge, I've adjusted the recipe to use simple syrup. It's more of a guideline than a recipe, so adjust the syrup level to find the right balance of tang and sweet.

To a pint glass, add the lime juice and Simple Syrup to taste and stir well. Add a handful of ice, then top with sparkling water and gently stir again. Taste to see if more syrup is needed. You may need up to 1 tablespoon (15 mL) more Simple Syrup.

MAKES 1 DRINK

moroccan mint limonana

½ cup (125 mL) sugar
½ cup (125 mL) lemon juice
¼ cup (60 mL) mint leaves
  (pulled from stems)
1 teaspoon (5 mL) orange
  blossom water (optional)
3 cups (750 mL) cold water,
  divided (approximately)

Travelling to Morocco in the fall a few years ago, I was expecting cooler temperatures, but even in October, the heat there can be stifling. Mint tea is refreshing, even as odd as it seems to drink hot tea in hot weather. But one afternoon my friend and I stopped for a drink at a restaurant in a little square near the souk in Essaouira, a small city on the western coast, and I ordered a mint lemonade. The icy and tangy lemonade made with cooling mint was better than a cool breeze. Find orange blossom water at Indian or Middle Eastern grocery stores.

In a blender or food processor, add the sugar, lemon juice, mint leaves, orange blossom water and 2 cups (500 mL) cold water. Blend until the mint is in tiny pieces and all the ingredients are well mixed, about a minute. Pour into a pitcher and add 1 cup (250 mL) more of water. Taste and add up to 1 cup (250 mL) more of cold water if the drink is too strong.

MAKES ABOUT 4 CUPS (1 L)

goat cheese with lemon and herb olive oil

½ cup (125 mL) extra virgin
   olive oil
peel of 1 lemon, in 1 long piece
   or several pieces
6 cloves garlic, thinly sliced
2 bay leaves
15 whole black peppercorns
2 tablespoons (30 mL) fresh
   rosemary (needles pulled
   from the stem)
½ teaspoon (2.5 mL)
   coriander seeds
8 ounces (250 g) goat cheese
zest of 1 lemon

Years ago, my mum used to make Anzac cookies from a photo-copy of a *Gourmet* recipe. On the same page was an appetizer recipe that called for infusing olive oil with herbs and spices and pouring it all over goat cheese. One Christmas Eve, she decided to make it for the family, and it quickly became a tradition to eat it with crusty baguette slices. We've slowly adapted it to suit our tastes, adding much more garlic and taking out some spices we didn't like. Then I began to experiment by adding lemon, which imparts a nice brightness to this rich appetizer.

In a small saucepan, warm the olive oil over medium-low heat. Remove as much of the bitter white pith from the lemon peel as possible and add the peel to the olive oil, letting it steep for about 15 minutes. The oil should not be hot enough to cook the peel or cause it to spatter. If it does, reduce the heat.

Add the garlic, bay leaves, peppercorns, rosemary and corian-der seeds and turn up the heat slightly, so small bubbles can be seen around the garlic and spices. Cook, stirring occasionally, until the garlic is soft and has lost some of its sharp taste and the oil is fragrant, about 5 minutes.

Slice the cheese into pieces about 1 inch (2.5 cm) thick (using a piece of unflavoured dental floss is the best way to do this) and set them in a serving dish. Spoon the oil, garlic and herbs over the cheese. Zest the second lemon on top.

Serve with crackers, bread or both.

SERVES 6 TO 8

baked ricotta with lemon and chives

2 cups (500 mL) ricotta

2 eggs, lightly beaten

zest of 1 lemon

1 clove garlic, minced

⅓ cup (80 mL) grated
  Parmesan

2 tablespoons (30 mL)
  chopped chives

⅛ teaspoon (0.5 mL) chili
  flakes

3 tablespoons (45 mL) extra
  virgin olive oil, divided

Smooth ricotta has a lot of uses, including as the basis for this hot spread, flavoured with a bit of chili and lemon zest for brightness. Ricotta is readily found at most stores, but is also incredibly easy to make. Find the recipe (page 206) in the Basics section.

Preheat the oven to 375°F (190°C). Butter either a small baking dish or 2 or more ramekins of any size that hold about 3 cups (750 mL) between them.

In a bowl, mix the ricotta, eggs, lemon zest, garlic, Parmesan, chives, chili flakes and 2 tablespoons (30 mL) of the olive oil. Stir until well combined. Spoon into the baking dish or ramekins and smooth the top. Bake until hot and slightly browned on top. The time will depend on the size of the baking dish or ramekins, but start checking at the 15-minute mark. Ricotta baked in deeper dishes will take longer.

Drizzle the last tablespoon of oil over the ricotta and serve with crackers or bread.

MAKES ABOUT 3 CUPS (750 ML)

lemon-thyme gougeres

1 cup (250 mL) water
6 tablespoons (90 mL)
  unsalted butter
½ teaspoon (2.5 mL) salt
freshly ground pepper
pinch nutmeg
¾ cup (185 mL) flour
4 eggs
2 tablespoons (30 mL) grated
  Parmesan
2 teaspoons (10 mL) fresh
  thyme leaves
zest of 1 lemon

These classic savoury French puffs get a tangy makeover with the addition of lemon zest and an herbal hit of thyme. Other herbs— parsley and rosemary, for example—would also be great. Since I'm not known for my patience, I've gone with a method that uses a stand mixer to beat in the eggs. Feel free to use the more conventional method of incorporating them using a wooden spoon.

Preheat the oven to 400°F (200°C) and line 2 baking sheets with parchment paper.

Add the water and the butter, salt, pepper and nutmeg to a medium saucepan, set over medium heat and bring to a boil, stirring until the butter has melted. Remove from the heat and immediately add all the flour, stirring quickly and vigorously with a wooden spoon until the dough forms a ball and is pulling away from the sides of the pot. Return the pot to the element and keep stirring until the dough is no longer sticky and forms a film on the bottom of the pot, about 1 or 2 minutes.

Tip the dough into the bowl of a stand mixer fitted with the paddle attachment and let cool for a minute or so. On medium speed, beat in the eggs, one at a time, letting each completely incorporate before adding the next one. Mix in the Parmesan, thyme and lemon zest.

Drop rounded teaspoons of dough onto the parchment-lined baking sheets, leaving about 2 inches (5 cm) between them. Dip your finger in a bit of water and press down any tips that are poking up.

Bake until golden brown, about 20 to 25 minutes. They should feel light and hollow, but the centres should still look moist. (Check by using a sharp paring knife to poke one open and then peering inside.)

Serve hot from the oven or after cooling slightly.

MAKES ABOUT 3 DOZEN GOUGERES, DEPENDING ON THEIR SIZE

meyer lemon focaccia

1½ teaspoons (7.5 mL) active
  dry yeast
1 teaspoon (5 mL) sugar
1¾ cups (435 mL) warm
  water, divided
3 cups (750 mL) flour
1½ teaspoons (7.5 mL) salt
5 tablespoons (75 mL) extra
  virgin olive oil, divided
  (approximately)
1 Meyer lemon, sliced thinly
flaked salt or fleur de sel for
  sprinkling

This is more like a cross between a focaccia and a pizza bianca. There's a little more chewiness than with a standard focaccia and the dough is much wetter, so this is best made with a stand mixer. Thin slices of Meyer lemon and a sprinkling of flaked salt add tang and saltiness, which works well with the oil-rich dough. The trick is to slice the Meyer lemon as thinly as possible, otherwise it can be quite tart. I use an incredibly sharp mandoline, which helps. But a good sharp knife will also work. Chill the lemon in the fridge to harden it up a bit before slicing.

In a small bowl, mix together the yeast, sugar and ¾ cup (185 mL) of warm water. Let the yeast bloom until creamy, about 10 minutes.

Add the flour and salt to the bowl of a stand mixer that has been fitted with the dough hook and pour in the yeast-water mixture along with the remaining 1 cup (250 mL) of water. On low speed, begin to mix together until no dry patches of flour remain, scraping down the side of the bowl as necessary. Add 2 tablespoons (30 mL) of olive oil and mix for another minute. Turn the mixer onto medium-high speed and let it knead the dough until it is shiny and has pulled away from the side of the bowl completely, leaving it bare, about 6 to 8 minutes. When the mixer stops, the dough should slide off the hook to the bottom of the bowl.

Add 1 tablespoon (15 mL) of olive oil to a large bowl, rubbing it up and down the side with your fingertips. Using your oiled fingers, transfer the dough from the mixer to the large bowl to rise. (The dough is incredibly sticky; the oil makes it easier to handle.) Cover with plastic wrap and let rise until doubled, about 1 to 1½ hours.

RECIPE CONTINUED ON NEXT PAGE

Line a baking sheet with a piece of parchment paper that hangs over the edges. Pour on 1 tablespoon (15 mL) of olive oil and spread all over the parchment that covers the pan. (There's no need to oil the overhang.) Tip the risen dough onto the prepared baking sheet and, using the tips of your fingers, stretch the dough to fill it, dimpling the surface as you go. If the dough resists, wait a few minutes and then continue. It will fill the baking sheet with a little patience.

Drizzle another tablespoon or two (15 to 30 mL) of olive oil over the dough, letting it fill the dimples. Cover loosely with plastic wrap and let it rise again for about 30 minutes.

As it rises, preheat the oven to 450°F (230°C).

Just before baking, scatter the slices of Meyer lemon overtop and sprinkle with a few pinches of flaked salt or fleur de sel. Bake until golden and cooked through, about 15 to 20 minutes.

Remove from the pan and serve warm. (Though, really, I would eat this at any temperature.)

MAKES 1 LARGE FOCACCIA

mixed olives with lemon, garlic and rosemary

3 tablespoons (45 mL) extra
   virgin olive oil
1 tablespoon (15 mL) fresh
   rosemary (needles pulled
   from the stem)
2 cloves garlic, thinly sliced
peel of half a lemon, julienned
2 cups (500 mL) assorted
   olives

I never used to like olives, which was great for my friend Julie, who always got to eat them whenever some ended up in front of us. But slowly I have begun to see the error of my ways. On a trip to Morocco together, she and I found ourselves both reaching for the small dishes of olives. These ones I've flavoured with some lemon peel, garlic and rosemary. I like to get an assortment of olives for different textures and colours.

In a small saucepan, warm the oil over medium-low heat, then add the rosemary, garlic and lemon peel. Cook until the garlic and peel have softened and the oil is fragrant, about 5 to 8 minutes. Add the olives and cook for a few minutes, stirring occasionally. Remove from the heat and let stand for at least 15 minutes before serving.

These can be made ahead of time and refrigerated, which will further infuse the olives with the flavour. Let warm to room temperature before serving.

MAKES ABOUT 2 CUPS (500 ML)

scallops with meyer lemon beurre blanc

12 large scallops

salt

freshly ground pepper

1 tablespoon (15 mL) extra
   virgin olive oil or vegetable
   oil

1 shallot, minced

½ cup (125 mL) white wine

2 tablespoons (30 mL) Meyer
   lemon juice

1½ teaspoons (7.5 mL)
   whipping cream

6 tablespoons (90 mL) butter,
   cut into 6 cubes

Tender scallops pair perfectly with a traditional beurre blanc tinged with sweet Meyer lemon juice. This dish works well as an appetizer or as part of a main course.

Using a paper towel, pat the scallops dry on both sides and then season all over with salt and pepper.

Set a heavy-bottomed pan over medium-high heat and add the oil. When the pan is hot and the oil is shimmering, add the scallops in batches, taking care not to crowd them. Sear until they have a nice golden crust—about 2 minutes—and then turn them over to sauté the other side for about a minute more. The scallops should still be slightly translucent in the centre. When they're cooked, set them aside on a plate.

While they are cooking, add the shallot, wine and lemon juice to a small saucepan and bring to a boil, cooking until the liquid has reduced by more than half. Turn the heat to low. Strain the liquid, then return it to the saucepan. Off the heat, stir in the cream and then whisk in the butter cubes, one at a time, only adding the next when the one before has disappeared. If the butter doesn't seem to be melting, move the saucepan back onto the heat to warm the mixture slightly.

Taste for seasonings, adding salt if desired.

Divide the scallops among 4 plates or place on a serving dish and drizzle with the beurre blanc.

SERVES 4 AS AN APPETIZER OR FEWER AS A MAIN COURSE

soups, salads
& sides

tom kha gai

4 cups (1 L) chicken stock

1 stalk lemongrass

4 kaffir lime leaves, fresh or dried (see note)

1 or 2 red chilies, cut into chunks

2 cloves garlic, crushed

one 3-inch (8 cm) piece of ginger, cut into 4 pieces

1 pound (500 g) boneless, skinless chicken breast, sliced ¼ inch (6 mm) thick

one 14-ounce (398 mL) can coconut milk

1 cup (250 mL) oyster mushrooms, torn (see note)

¼ cup (60 mL) lime juice

2 tablespoons (30 mL) fish sauce

1½ teaspoons (7.5 mL) brown sugar

cilantro

chili oil

lime wedges

When my sisters and I get together for dinner, we often end up at a Thai restaurant where we always have to order this soup, along with chicken skewers and peanut satay sauce. The creamy coconut broth is punched up with chili and lots of lime, and I love to drizzle chili oil overtop just before eating for little pockets of more heat.

In a saucepan set over high heat, bring the stock to a boil. Cut off the tough end of the lemongrass stalk, then, using the back of a knife, bruise the lemongrass. Cut into pieces a few inches long. Add the lemongrass, lime leaves, chilies, garlic and ginger to the stock and reduce the heat. Cover with a lid and let simmer for about 10 minutes to let all the flavours infuse the stock.

Remove the aromatics. Add the chicken and continue to simmer until it's cooked, about 5 minutes. Add the coconut milk, oyster mushrooms, lime juice, fish sauce and brown sugar. Bring back to a simmer until everything is hot and the mushrooms are slightly softened.

Serve with cilantro (either coarsely chopped or left whole), chili oil and lime wedges.

SERVES 4 ALONG WITH OTHER DISHES OR 2 AS A MAIN COURSE

Kaffir lime leaves are fragrant leaves that impart a lime flavour to the soup. They can typically be found at Asian markets. The peel from half a lime can be used instead.
Regular button mushrooms can be substituted for oyster mushrooms, but need a bit more time to cook. Add them at the same time as the chicken.

curry-lime lentil soup with yogurt and mango chutney

1 tablespoon (15 mL)
   vegetable oil
1 medium yellow onion, diced
salt
2 cloves garlic, minced
1 teaspoon (5 mL) minced
   fresh ginger
2 teaspoons (10 mL) curry
   powder
¼ teaspoon (1 mL) turmeric
¼ teaspoon (1 mL) chili flakes
   (optional)
4 cups (1 L) chicken or
   vegetable stock
1½ cups (375 mL) red lentils
juice of 2 limes, divided
⅔ cup (160 mL) yogurt
¼ cup (60 mL) mango
   chutney
freshly ground pepper
lime wedges

Growing up, I had the luxury of getting to eat lots of homemade curries thanks to a stepdad who made his own spice combinations and concoctions, resulting in fiery dishes I'd need to cool with yogurt. This soup takes those flavours and adds in the tang of lime and some sweet and spicy mango chutney.

Set a saucepan over medium heat and add the oil. When the oil is hot, add the onion and a pinch or two of salt. Sauté the onions until translucent and soft but not brown, about 5 minutes. Add the garlic and ginger and cook until the garlic is fragrant, about 1 minute. Add the curry powder, turmeric and chili flakes, if using. Stir well until the spices have coated the onions and garlic and have toasted slightly, about 1 to 2 minutes. Pour in the stock and scrape up any of the spices that are coating the bottom of the saucepan. Let the stock come to a boil and then add the lentils. Stir well, then reduce the heat to a simmer and cover with a lid, cooking until the lentils are soft, about 15 to 20 minutes.

While the soup cooks, prepare the yogurt topping. In a small bowl, mix together 2 tablespoons (30 mL) lime juice, the yogurt and the mango chutney. Set aside until the soup is ready to serve. (This can be made in advance and refrigerated.)

When the lentils are completely soft and the soup has thickened, use a hand blender (or a standard one) to purée about half the soup. Season with more salt and with freshly ground pepper. Add most of the remaining lime juice. Taste for seasonings, adding more salt, pepper or lime juice as necessary.

Spoon into 4 bowls and top with a dollop of the yogurt mango chutney topping. Serve with lime wedges.

SERVES 4

peanut soup

2 tablespoons (30 mL)
  vegetable oil
1 small onion, finely diced
½ teaspoon (2.5 mL) salt,
  divided
3 cloves garlic, minced
1 teaspoon (5 mL) minced
  fresh ginger
2 tablespoons (30 mL) tomato
  paste
one 28-ounce (796 mL) can
  diced tomatoes
3 cups (750 mL) chicken stock
1 cup (250 mL) smooth peanut
  butter
¼ teaspoon (1 mL) freshly
  ground pepper
3 green onions, thinly sliced
½ cup (125 mL) roasted
  peanuts, coarsely chopped,
  plus more for serving
1 tablespoon (15 mL) Tabasco
  sauce
juice of 2 limes
lime wedges

A friend of mine made a version of this soup for me years ago and I immediately asked for the recipe. The combination of tomato and peanut butter is odd on paper but beautiful in the bowl. I've adapted it since then, adding tomato paste to intensify the tomato flavour, including ginger for some complexity and increasing the lime to cut the richness. It's rich and creamy, but the lime juice and Tabasco sauce keep it from tasting too heavy.

Set a large saucepan over medium heat and add the oil. Once heated, add the diced onion and half the salt. Sauté until the onion is soft and translucent, about 5 minutes. Add the minced garlic and ginger, then sauté for about a minute, until fragrant. Stir in the tomato paste and cook for another minute before pouring in the diced tomatoes and the chicken stock. Raise the heat and let the soup come to a simmer before adding the peanut butter. Stir thoroughly, waiting for the peanut butter to melt into the soup before covering and reducing the temperature to medium-low. Let the soup simmer for about 15 minutes.

Add the rest of the salt and the pepper, green onions, peanuts and Tabasco sauce. Add most of the lime juice and taste the soup. If it still tastes a bit rich or bland, add the rest of the lime juice and a bit more Tabasco sauce, as desired.

Serve with lime wedges, Tabasco sauce and roasted peanuts.

SERVES 4

avgolemono

8 cups (2 L) chicken or
  vegetable stock
1 cup (250 mL) orzo pasta or
  arborio rice
4 eggs, separated
zest of 1 lemon
juice of 3 lemons, strained
1½ teaspoon (7.5 mL) salt
¼ teaspoon (1 mL) freshly
  ground pepper

One of the best soups that can be whipped up with a few standard ingredients most of us regularly have on hand, this Greek dish gets a creamy texture from eggs and a bright flavour from lots of lemon. The trick here is to temper the eggs with hot stock so you don't end up with scrambled egg soup.

In a large saucepan, bring the stock to a boil over high heat. Add the orzo or rice and cook until just tender, about 6 or 7 minutes for the pasta and 15 to 20 minutes for the rice.

Meanwhile, in the bowl of a stand mixer fitted with a whisk attachment, whip the egg whites on medium-high speed until they form soft peaks. Add the yolks, lemon zest and juice and beat again until everything is just mixed but not so long that the whites begin to deflate.

Once the pasta or rice is cooked, take 2 cups (500 mL) of the stock from the pot. While beating the egg mixture on low to medium speed, add the stock in a very slow and steady stream, to temper the eggs, until the stock is fully incorporated. Take the soup off the heat and whisk in the egg mixture. Season with salt and pepper, then taste and add more seasonings or lemon if necessary.

Serve immediately.

SERVES 4

carrot ribbon salad with lime dressing

1 pound (500 g) carrots
1 avocado, sliced
¼ cup (60 mL) pistachios
¼ cup (60 mL) dried
  cranberries

DRESSING
2 tablespoons (30 mL) lime
  juice
1½ teaspoons (7.5 mL) sugar
¾ teaspoon (4 mL) salt
freshly ground pepper
3 tablespoons (45 mL) extra
  virgin olive oil

Using carrots in a variety of colours makes for a gorgeous salad, but the regular orange ones are just as tasty. The pistachios add a great crunch, while the cranberries play up the carrots' sweetness. Even friends and family who don't like carrots say they enjoy this salad.

Peel the carrots and then, using the peeler, lightly shave off layers of carrot in ribbons. In a bowl, mix the carrots, avocado slices, pistachios and cranberries.

In a jar with a lid or in a bowl, combine the lime juice, sugar, salt and pepper to taste. Give it a couple of shakes, or whisk together, and then add the oil. Shake or whisk again until emulsified. Pour a few tablespoons over the salad and toss lightly to keep the avocado from getting too mushy. Add more dressing as needed.

SERVES 2 TO 4

pink grapefruit and avocado salad with chili

2 ripe avocados, chilled
2 pink grapefruits, chilled
1 small fresh red chili

DRESSING
1 teaspoon (5 mL) cider
   vinegar or white wine
   vinegar
¾ teaspoon (4 mL) sugar
½ teaspoon (2.5 mL) grainy
   mustard
¼ teaspoon (1 mL) salt
1 tablespoon (15 mL)
   vegetable oil

I'm confident this is the strangest recipe in the book. After I sent it to my friend Katherine to try, she admitted she had hesitated to make it because it seemed too odd. But, after giving it a go, all doubts about the unusual combination were gone. The cooling avocados, tangy grapefruits and spicy chili work unexpectedly well together.

Cut the avocados in half, take out the pits, and gently remove the peels. Slice each half into pieces about ¼-inch (6 mm) thick. With a sharp knife, cut the skin and all the pith off the grapefruits by following the curve of the fruit. Then, over a bowl to catch the juice, cut the segments of the grapefruits between the membranes, releasing the pieces. Squeeze the remaining juice into the bowl and set aside. Remove the seeds and membranes from the chili and dice finely. (You may not need all of the chili, depending on how spicy the chili is and your tolerance for heat. Mine is quite low, so I use about half.)

Divide the avocado slices and grapefruit segments among plates and sprinkle with a bit of the diced chili, about ⅛ teaspoon (0.5 mL) or more, if desired.

To make the dressing, add 2 teaspoons (10 mL) of reserved grapefruit juice and the vinegar, sugar, mustard and salt to a jar with a lid or to a bowl. Shake or whisk until the sugar has dissolved, then add the oil, shake or slowly whisk it in to emulsify the dressing, and drizzle over the salads.

SERVES 2 TO 4

shaved brussels sprout salad with lemon dressing

3 cups (750 mL) Brussels
  sprouts (about 15 to
  20 medium ones)
2 shallots, peeled
⅓ cup (80 mL) sliced almonds,
  toasted and cooled

DRESSING
3 tablespoons (45 mL) lemon
  juice
2 tablespoons (30 mL) grainy
  mustard
1 tablespoon (15 mL) cider
  vinegar
1 tablespoon (15 mL) sugar
salt
freshly ground pepper
½ cup (125 mL) vegetable oil

The rule in my family is everyone at Christmas must consume at least one boiled Brussels sprout. I'm the only one who resists and tries to work around it or, at a minimum, drown it in gravy. In the last few years, I've made it my mission to learn to appreciate these little vegetables, ultimately discovering how much I like them sautéed with pasta or served raw in a salad like this one. If you have a mandoline, this salad comes together very quickly, but it won't take too much longer without.

If using a mandoline, hold the stem end of each Brussels sprout and shave into a bowl, stopping when you get close to the stem and slices of the hard core of the sprout start to show up. Repeat with the 2 shallots, shaving down to the root. (If using a knife, hold the Brussels sprout stem and cut as thinly as possible until the core of the sprout shows up. Repeat with the shallots.) In a bowl, toss the shaved sprouts and shallots lightly, then add the almonds.

Make the dressing by adding the lemon juice, mustard, vinegar, sugar and salt and pepper to taste to a jar with a lid or to a bowl, then shaking or whisking well to mix. Add the oil and shake or whisk again until emulsified. Taste for seasonings, adding more salt and pepper as needed.

Pour most of the dressing over the salad and toss. Add more dressing as needed.

SERVES 4

asparagus salad with parmesan and lemon-dijon dressing

1 bunch asparagus
(about 1 pound [500 g])

4 to 5 green onions, sliced

1 cup (250 mL) grated
Parmesan

½ cup (125 mL) walnuts,
toasted and coarsely
chopped

DRESSING

2 tablespoons (30 mL) lemon
juice

2 teaspoons (10 mL) Dijon
mustard

1 teaspoon (5 mL) honey

½ teaspoon (2.5 mL) salt

½ teaspoon (2.5 mL) freshly
ground pepper

2 tablespoons (30 mL) extra
virgin olive oil

Roasted, grilled, steamed—I like asparagus in all forms, but especially raw in a salad. The tangy lemon dressing, spiked with mustard, makes this salad really bright, while the walnuts add a pleasing crunch.

Chop off the rough ends of the asparagus and then slice crosswise into ¼-inch (6 mm) coins, leaving the tips intact. In a large bowl, combine the chopped asparagus, green onions, Parmesan and walnuts.

In a jar with a lid or in a small bowl, combine the lemon juice, Dijon mustard, honey, salt and pepper. Shake or whisk to mix thoroughly, then add the oil and shake or whisk again until the dressing has emulsified. Pour most of the dressing over the salad and toss. Add more dressing as needed. Serve immediately.

SERVES 4

biryani-style quinoa salad with curry-lime dressing

4 cups (1 L) cooked quinoa,
   cooled
2 small zucchini, julienned
4 to 6 carrots (about
   ½ pound [250 g]), julienned
4 green onions, sliced
1½ cups (375 mL) canned
   chickpeas, drained and
   rinsed (one 14-ounce
   [398 mL] can)
1 cup (250 mL) currants

DRESSING
zest and juice of 2 limes
2 tablespoons (30 mL) honey
1 teaspoon (5 mL) salt
1 teaspoon (5 mL) curry
   powder
½ teaspoon (2.5 mL) ground
   ginger
½ teaspoon (2.5 mL) ground
   cinnamon
¼ cup (60 mL) vegetable oil

Sometimes a phrase is enough to get the culinary ideas flowing. In this case, the mention of the word biryani—the rice-based dish that uses spices like cinnamon, ginger and nutmeg—got me thinking about making a salad using those Indian flavours. I added carrots for crunch and currants for sweetness. The honey-and-lime dressing brings it all together.

In a large bowl, combine the cooked and cooled quinoa, julienned zucchini and carrots, green onions, chickpeas and currants.

In a jar with a lid or in a small bowl, zest the 2 limes and squeeze in their juice. Drizzle in the honey and shake or whisk until it has dissolved. Add the salt, curry powder, ginger and cinnamon and shake or whisk until the salt has also dissolved. Add the oil and shake or whisk again until emulsified. Pour most of the dressing over the salad and toss. Add more dressing as needed. This can be served immediately or made ahead and refrigerated, then served chilled.

SERVES 4

quinoa tabbouleh

4 cups (1 L) cooked quinoa,
  cooled
1 red, orange or yellow
  pepper, diced
2 to 4 green onions, thinly
  sliced
2 mini cucumbers, halved,
  seeded and sliced
1 cup (250 mL) cherry or
  grape tomatoes, halved or
  quartered
¼ cup (60 mL) mint, chopped
¼ cup (60 mL) parsley,
  chopped

DRESSING
⅓ cup (80 mL) lemon juice
  (from about 2 lemons)
1 teaspoon (5 mL) salt
freshly ground pepper
⅓ cup (80 mL) extra virgin
  olive oil

I never order tabbouleh anywhere because I just don't love bulgur, the grain traditionally used in this Middle Eastern salad. When I impulse-bought a giant bag of quinoa and was looking for ways to use it up, it occurred to me to use some of that grain instead. The lemon dressing, along with the herbs, makes this taste incredibly fresh and clean.

In a large bowl, combine the cooked and cooled quinoa, red pepper, green onions, cucumbers, tomatoes, mint and parsley.

In a jar with a lid or in a separate bowl, mix lemon juice, salt and pepper to taste. Shake or whisk to dissolve the salt. Add the oil and shake or whisk again until emulsified. Pour most of the dressing over the salad and toss. Add more dressing as needed. Serve immediately.

SERVES 4

southwest salad with honey-lime dressing

6 cups (1.5 L) romaine lettuce, chopped (1 large head)
one 14-ounce (398 mL) can black beans, drained and rinsed
1 cup (250 mL) corn (see note)
1 cup (250 mL) pitted dates, roughly chopped
4 ounces (125 g) feta, crumbled
2 avocados, diced

DRESSING
juice of 1 lime
1½ tablespoons (22.5 mL) honey
¼ teaspoon (1 mL) salt
¼ teaspoon (1 mL) freshly ground pepper
⅓ cup (80 mL) vegetable oil (approximately)

Years ago, a restaurant I sometimes went to served a salad that brought together the unexpected combination of southwestern US flavours like avocado, black beans and corn with more exotic feta and dates. I couldn't get enough of it. A couple of years ago, after reminiscing with my friend Kirsten about the salad—as she had been as enamoured with it as I was—I decided to come up with my own version. I knew I'd nailed it when we ate it for dinner one night and she finished the entire thing straight from the serving bowl.

In a large bowl, combine the lettuce, black beans, corn, dates, feta and avocados.

In a jar with a lid or in a separate bowl, mix the lime juice and honey. Shake or whisk until the honey has dissolved, then add the salt and pepper. Add most of the oil and give it all a good shake or whisk until the dressing has emulsified. Taste for seasonings. If the dressing is too tart, add the rest of the oil.

Pour most of the dressing over the salad and toss. Add more dressing as needed. Serve immediately.

SERVES 4

I usually use frozen corn here, thawing and draining it before adding it to the salad. Canned corn will also work, or fresh corn that has been blanched and cut off the cob.

chicken and rice vermicelli salad with herbs and lime

8 ounces (250 g) rice
  vermicelli
1 pound (500 g) cooked
  chicken, sliced or shredded
2 carrots, julienned
½ red pepper, julienned
1 fat red chili, seeded and
  sliced or diced
½ cup (125 mL) snow peas, cut
  thinly on a diagonal
½ cup (125 mL) fresh herbs
  (such as a combination of
  basil, mint and cilantro),
  coarsely chopped, divided

DRESSING
1 clove garlic, grated
zest of 2 limes
⅓ cup (80 mL) lime juice
¼ cup (60 mL) brown sugar
¼ cup (60 mL) fish sauce
2 teaspoon (10 mL) chili paste
  (such as sambal oelek)

This is an incredibly light dish, ideal for eating out on a patio, just shaded from the summer sun. The level of spice works for me—a well-known wimp when it comes to chili heat—so feel free to bump it up by adding more chili paste to the dressing or more fresh ones to the salad itself. I usually use two sautéed chicken breasts that I thinly slice before adding to the salad, but this is also a great way to use up any leftover cooked chicken you have around.

Set a large pot of water over high heat and bring to a boil. Once at a full rolling boil, add the vermicelli noodles, stir lightly and turn off the heat. Let sit until tender, about 3 to 4 minutes, then drain and rinse with cold water. Add to a large bowl—ideally the one you will want to serve from. Mix in the cooked chicken, carrots, red pepper, chili, snow peas and fresh herbs, reserving a tablespoon or so of herbs to sprinkle over the salad at the end.

In a jar with a lid or in a small bowl, shake or whisk together the garlic, lime zest and juice, brown sugar, fish sauce and chili paste. Taste for seasonings, adding more lime or chili if desired. Drizzle the dressing over the salad and toss gently until all the noodles and vegetables are coated. Sprinkle the rest of the chopped herbs overtop and serve.

SERVES 4

thai beef slaw

8 ounces (250 g) flank steak
1 tablespoon (15 mL)
 vegetable oil
salt
freshly ground pepper
¼ cup (60 mL) peanuts,
 coarsely chopped (optional)

SALAD
4 cups (1 L) shredded cabbage
 (about a ½ pound [250 g])
2 carrots, julienned
3 to 4 green onions, sliced
½ red pepper, thinly sliced
¼ cup (60 mL) cilantro,
 coarsely chopped
¼ cup (60 mL) mint, coarsely
 chopped

DRESSING
1 clove garlic, minced
¼ cup (60 mL) lime juice
1½ tablespoons (22.5 mL) fish
 sauce
1 tablespoon (15 mL) brown
 sugar
1 tablespoon (15 mL) minced
 fresh ginger
½ teaspoon (2.5 mL) chili
 paste
½ teaspoon (2.5 mL) sesame
 oil

Inspired by Thai ingredients, I wanted to put together a salad full of flavour and crisp freshness. The result is a crunchy slaw with tender beef and a zingy dressing that's sour, spicy, salty and sweet.

Set a grill or cast iron pan over medium-high heat and let it get hot while you prepare the steak by brushing both sides with the oil and seasoning liberally with salt and freshly ground pepper. When the pan is hot, sear the steak for 2 to 3 minutes on each side for medium rare (add another minute or two for medium), then remove to a cutting board and let the meat rest while preparing the rest of the salad.

In a large bowl, add the cabbage, carrots, green onions, red pepper and herbs. Toss lightly.

In a jar with a lid or in a small bowl, mix together the garlic, lime juice, fish sauce, brown sugar, ginger, chili paste and sesame oil. Pour most of the dressing over the salad and toss. Add more dressing as needed.

After the beef has rested, carve slices as thin as possible and add to the salad, tossing it all together. Top with chopped peanuts, if desired.

SERVES 4

grilled new york steak and grapefruit salad

one 10-ounce (300 g) New
   York steak
½ teaspoon (2.5 mL) extra
   virgin olive oil
½ teaspoon (2.5 mL) Montreal
   steak spice
1 grapefruit
2 cups (500 mL) chopped
   romaine lettuce
½ cup (125 mL) arugula
¼ cucumber, peeled, halved
   seeded and sliced
4 cherry tomatoes, halved
4 radishes, thinly sliced
⅛ red onion, thinly sliced
1 tablespoon (15 mL) each dill,
   tarragon and basil, chopped

DRESSING

2 tablespoons (30 mL) cider
   vinegar
½ teaspoon (2.5 mL) honey
zest from ½ lemon
salt
freshly ground pepper
3 tablespoons (45 mL) extra
   virgin olive oil

It is an odd combination of ingredients, but this salad from Chef Liana Robberecht of Calgary is so beloved by her friends that several mentioned it to me on separate occasions, raving about how good it is. Once I tried it myself, I understood why. The chopped romaine can be augmented with other greens, like frisée.

Set a grill or cast iron pan over medium-high heat and let it get hot while you prepare the steak by brushing both sides with the oil and pressing in the steak spice. Once the pan is hot, cook the steak to medium rare or desired doneness, turning once. Remove to a plate and let rest for 5 to 7 minutes.

With a sharp knife, cut the skin and all the pith off the grapefruit by following the curve of the fruit. Then, over a bowl to catch the juice, cut the segments of the grapefruit between the membranes, releasing the pieces. Squeeze the remaining juice into the bowl and set aside.

Divide the lettuce, arugula, cucumber, tomatoes, radishes, red onion and herbs between 2 plates. Top each with half the grapefruit segments.

In a jar with a lid or in a small bowl, mix together the reserved grapefruit juice, vinegar, honey, lemon zest and salt and pepper to taste. Shake or whisk until the honey has dissolved. Add the oil and shake or whisk again until the dressing has emulsified. Drizzle over the salads. Slice the steak thinly and divide between the 2 plates, placing atop the salad. Serve immediately.

SERVES 2

lemon-thyme soubise

½ cup (125 mL) arborio rice

¼ cup (60 mL) unsalted
  butter

2 pounds (1 kg) onions,
  trimmed, peeled
  and sliced very thin
  (about 5 to 6 medium-sized
  onions)

3 sprigs thyme, divided

½ teaspoon (2.5 mL) salt

freshly ground pepper

½ cup (125 mL) freshly grated
  Parmesan

¼ cup (60 mL) whipping
  cream

2 tablespoons (30 mL) lemon
  juice

I had never heard of soubise until my friend Katherine asked if I was thinking of including a version in this book. It turns out she's been making numerous versions of the rice and onion casserole dish from Julia Child for a long time. Among those adaptations is this lemon and thyme one, which she shared with me. She recommends serving it with chicken or white fish and notes it can be made ahead of time and reheated just before serving.

Preheat the oven to 300°F (150°C).

In a medium pot, bring 2 cups (500 mL) salted water to a boil and add the rice. Cook it for exactly 5 minutes and then immediately drain.

In a large casserole dish (or heavy-bottomed skillet that has a lid) set over medium heat, melt the butter. When it starts to foam, add the onions and sauté until softened and translucent, about 5 to 10 minutes. Add the rice, 2 of the thyme sprigs, and the salt and pepper to taste. Stir well, cover and put in the oven to bake for an hour, stirring once or twice. (If the rice is still a little underdone, return to the oven for another 10 to 30 minutes.)

Remove and discard the thyme sprigs. Stir in the grated cheese, cream and lemon juice. Remove the thyme leaves from the last sprig and stir them into the dish.

SERVES 4 TO 6

barley risotto with lemon, leeks and peas

3 cups (750 mL) chicken stock

2 tablespoons (30 mL) extra virgin olive oil

1 tablespoon (15 mL) butter

3 medium leeks, white and pale green parts thinly sliced, rinsed and drained

½ teaspoon (2.5 mL) salt

3 cloves garlic, minced

1 cup (250 mL) pearl barley

½ cup (125 mL) dry white wine

¾ cup (185 mL) fresh or frozen peas

2 tablespoons (30 mL) whipping cream

zest of 1 lemon

½ to 1 tablespoon (7.5 to 15 mL) lemon juice

½ cup (125 mL) grated Parmesan, plus more for sprinkling

It may be cheeky to call this a risotto since the traditional version uses rice, but the cooking technique is the same. The barley gets just as creamy as it cooks slowly with broth, but still stays a bit chewy for a much heartier dish. I like this with a lot of lemon zip, so I add the full tablespoon of lemon juice. Sprinkle some roughly chopped basil overtop just before serving for a bit more green and a herbal hit. This dish is excellent with roasted or pan-seared chicken.

In a small saucepan set over medium heat, bring the chicken stock to a low simmer. Keep it barely simmering as you prepare the risotto.

In a large saucepan set over medium heat, warm the oil and butter until the butter starts to foam slightly. Add the leeks and salt and sauté, stirring occasionally, until the leeks are softened, 2 to 3 minutes, then add the garlic and cook until it's fragrant, about a minute more. Stir in the pearl barley, mixing it with the leeks and garlic until each grain is coated and shimmering with the oil and butter and is slightly toasted, about 2 to 3 minutes. Pour in the white wine and stir until most of it is absorbed.

Begin adding the simmering stock, about ½ a cup (125 mL) at a time, stirring often and waiting until most of the liquid has been absorbed before adding more. It should take 4 to 5 minutes for the barley to soak up the liquid between additions. If it's taking a lot less time than that, reduce the heat. If it's taking more, turn up the heat.

Just after the last bit of stock has been added, stir in the peas. Add the cream, lemon zest, ½ a tablespoon (7.5 mL) of lemon juice and the Parmesan, then stir gently until everything is mixed together. Taste for seasonings, and add the rest of the lemon juice if desired. Sprinkle with additional Parmesan just before serving.

SERVES 4 AS A SIDE DISH OR 2 AS A MAIN COURSE

roasted lemon potatoes with garlic and oregano

3 pounds (1.5 kg) Yukon gold or baking potatoes, peeled and cut into 1½-inch (4 cm) pieces

½ cup (125 mL) extra virgin olive oil or canola oil

4 cloves garlic, crushed or thinly sliced

1½ teaspoons (7.5 mL) dried oregano, crumbled

1 teaspoon (5 mL) salt

freshly ground pepper

½ cup (125 ml) beef or chicken stock

⅓ cup (80 ml) lemon juice

fresh oregano, chopped (optional)

Cookbook author Julie Van Rosendaal suggested this recipe to me as an excellent side dish. The potatoes get tons of flavour from the garlic, oregano and lemon juice, making them a great addition to most meals. Other chopped herbs, like parsley or chives, can be tossed over the cooked potatoes at the end, besides the oregano, while another dusting of lemon zest at the end adds even more zip.

Preheat the oven to 400°F (200°C).

In a 9- × 13-inch (23 × 33 cm) baking dish, spread the potatoes in a single layer and drizzle the oil over them. Add the garlic, dried oregano, salt and pepper to taste and toss well to coat the potatoes with the oil. Bake the potatoes for 15 minutes, then add the stock, stirring to coat the potatoes, and bake for 10 minutes more. Add the lemon juice, stirring it all again, and bake for an additional 10 to 15 minutes, or until the potatoes are golden and cooked through. Sprinkle with fresh oregano, or other herbs, if desired, and serve.

SERVES 4 TO 6

main dishes

spaghetti al limone

1 pound (500 g) spaghetti (or another long noodle, like linguine)

2 lemons, zested, juiced and strained, divided

1 egg yolk

⅓ cup (80 mL) whipping cream

3 tablespoons (45 mL) extra virgin olive oil

1 cup (250 mL) grated Parmesan, divided

freshly ground pepper

salt (optional)

2 to 3 tablespoons (30 to 45 mL) parsley, coarsely chopped

It sounds much more exotic and interesting than lemon spaghetti—more authentic too—but the truth is that a straight-forward name probably better reflects the simplicity of this pasta dish. I found versions of it that required cooking the cream first or called for other extra steps. In this one, whisk a few ingredients, pour over hot pasta and toss, toss, toss. That's the sum total of it. At the end, it's a creamy tangle of pasta, each strand coated in a rich, lemony sauce. Add some freshly ground pepper for a bit of heat and parsley for freshness at the end for a well-rounded pasta dish.

Bring a large pot of water to a boil over high heat, salt heavily and add the pasta, cooking until al dente. (Start checking the pasta a minute or two before the package instructions suggest it will be cooked.)

In a small bowl, whisk together the lemon zest, egg yolk, cream, olive oil and ¾ cup (185 mL) Parmesan. Add a few grinds of pepper and make sure it's all well mixed. Pour in about ¼ cup (60 mL) of the lemon juice and mix again.

When the pasta is cooked just al dente—there should still be a bit of chewiness to it—scoop out 1 cup (250 mL) of the cooking liquid before draining the pasta. Return the pasta to the pot and add about ¼ cup (60 mL) of the reserved pasta water. Toss the pasta (I find tongs are best for this part) so it's coated with the cooking liquid, adding more if the noodles still seem dry. Pour the cream–lemon juice mixture over the pasta and toss and stir, getting it well mixed. The heat of the pasta will cook the egg yolk and melt the cheese to create a creamy sauce. Add more pasta water if it seems a bit dry or the sauce isn't coating all the noodles. Taste for seasonings, splashing on more lemon juice, if desired, or salt, if needed.

Serve sprinkled with the remaining grated Parmesan, chopped parsley and more pepper.

SERVES 4

linguine with tuna and lemon

12 ounces (375 g) linguine (see note)

2 tablespoons (30 mL) extra virgin olive oil

2 cloves garlic, thinly sliced

¼ teaspoon (1 mL) chili flakes

two 5½-ounce (156 mL) cans tuna packed in oil, drained (or cans totalling approximately 12 ounces [335 mL])

zest and juice of 1 lemon

¼ teaspoon (1 mL) salt

freshly ground pepper

1½ cups (375 mL) arugula

This is one of those ridiculously easy recipes that are excellent to have in your back pocket on nights when you just want something simple and delicious. I always keep a few cans of tuna packed in oil in my cupboard for just those occasions. The tuna has much more flavour than standard canned stuff; find it at Italian grocery stores.

Bring a large pot of water to a boil over high heat, salt heavily and add the pasta, cooking until it's al dente. (Start checking the pasta a minute or two before the package instructions suggest it will be cooked.)

While the pasta is cooking, set a small pan over medium heat and add the olive oil and sliced garlic at the same time, just cooking the garlic until it is soft and slightly translucent. Don't let it burn or get too golden. Add the chili flakes and cook another minute before removing from the heat and setting aside.

In a large serving bowl, combine the tuna, lemon zest and juice, salt and pepper to taste. Pour the garlic and oil over the tuna and toss it all together with a fork.

When the pasta is cooked just al dente—there should still be a bit of chewiness to it—reserve some of the cooking water before draining. Add the pasta to the tuna and lemon mixture, tossing it all together. Add a splash of the reserved cooking water if the dish seems a bit dry or hard to mix. Taste for seasonings, adding more salt or pepper as necessary. Sprinkle the arugula on top, lightly toss and serve.

SERVES 4

Although I call for linguine here, I've also used fettucine and spaghetti. A flatter noodle is best, but others can be substituted.

pasta with prosciutto, peas, mint
and lemon

8 ounces (250 g) small pasta, such as farfalle, penne or orecchiette
1 cup (250 mL) peas, fresh or frozen
3 tablespoons (45 mL) extra virgin olive oil
zest of 2 lemons
2 tablespoons (30 mL) lemon juice
1 teaspoon (5 mL) sugar
freshly ground pepper
3 tablespoons (45 mL) mint leaves
½ cup (125 mL) finely grated Parmesan, plus more for serving
4 ounces (125 g) prosciutto, cut or torn into thin strips
lemon wedges

Prosciutto and peas are the basis of one of my favourite pasta dishes. Peas and mint go together perfectly. And lemon? Well, it just brings everything together in this quick and easy pasta dish.

Bring a large pot of water to a boil over high heat, salt heavily and add the pasta. Cook until it is al dente (there should still be a slight chew to it), adding the fresh or frozen peas to the pot when the pasta is almost done. (Start checking the pasta a minute or two before the package instructions suggest it will be cooked.)

Meanwhile, in a large bowl—ideally the one you want to serve the pasta from—add the olive oil, lemon zest and juice, sugar and pepper to taste. Mix thoroughly. Stack the mint leaves and roll like a cigar, then slice into thin strips and stir into the lemon–olive oil mixture.

When the pasta is cooked, drain, reserving about ½ a cup (125 mL) of the cooking liquid. Add the drained pasta to the bowl and toss thoroughly. Sprinkle the Parmesan over the pasta and toss again, then add the prosciutto. If the mixture seems too dry, add a splash of the reserved pasta water and toss again.

Serve with a few lemon wedges and extra Parmesan for sprinkling over.

SERVES 4

cheese pizzas with herb salad and lemon dressing

DOUGH

1 cup (250 mL) warm water

2 teaspoons (10 mL) active dry yeast

1 teaspoon (5 mL) sugar

2¾ cups (685 mL) flour (approximately)

2 tablespoons (30 mL) extra virgin olive oil, divided

1 teaspoon (5 mL) salt

LEMON-GARLIC OIL

¼ cup (60 mL) extra virgin olive oil

peel of ½ lemon

2 to 3 cloves garlic, thinly sliced

DRESSING

2 tablespoons (30 mL) lemon juice

1 teaspoon (5 mL) sugar

½ teaspoon (2.5 mL) salt

freshly ground pepper

¼ cup (60 mL) extra virgin olive oil

PIZZA TOPPINGS

8 ounces (250 g) fresh mozzarella, pulled into strands

½ cup (125 mL) grated Parmesan

3½ cups (875 mL) spring mix salad

½ cup (125 mL) mixed herbs (basil, cilantro, dill, parsley—whatever you prefer or have on hand)

Hot bread and melty cheese, a swipe of garlic- and lemon-flavoured oil, topped with a salad permeated with fresh herbs and a tangy lemon dressing: that pretty much hits all the high notes for me. Barefoot Contessa Ina Garten has a pizza recipe that calls for arugula and lemon vinaigrette, which I've made a few times and enjoyed. But when I had neither goat cheese nor fontina nor arugula, I began to make my own amended version. I like to use spring mix salad (also known as mesclun or baby greens) and add a few handfuls of herbs for a bright, fresh flavour. There are prepackaged versions of this, which is handy, but it's equally easy to make your own.

In the bowl of a stand mixer, combine the water, yeast and sugar and stir gently once or twice. Let the yeast bloom until creamy, about 10 minutes.

Add the flour to the bowl and, using the paddle attachment, begin to mix together until no dry patches of flour remain. Add half the olive oil and the salt and mix for another minute. Switch to a dough hook, turn the mixer onto medium speed and let it knead the dough until it is shiny and smooth, about 7 minutes. (If the dough seems too wet and tacky, add up to another ¼ cup [60 mL] of flour, about a tablespoon [15 mL] at a time.)

Add the remaining tablespoon (15 mL) of olive oil to a large bowl, rubbing it up and down the side with your fingertips. Using your oiled fingers, transfer the dough to the bowl and turn to coat. Cover with plastic wrap and set aside somewhere warm until the dough has doubled in size, about 1 hour.

RECIPE CONTINUED ON NEXT PAGE

While the dough is rising, prepare the lemon-garlic oil. In a small pan set over medium-low heat, add the oil, lemon peel and sliced garlic. Cook, stirring occasionally, until the garlic has softened and is barely golden and the peel has started to go translucent. Turn off the heat and set aside.

Make the dressing by combining the lemon juice, sugar, salt and pepper in a jar with a lid or in a small bowl. Shake or whisk until the sugar and salt have dissolved, then add the oil and shake or whisk again until emulsified.

Preheat the oven to 450°F (230°C). Line 2 baking sheets with parchment paper. Divide the dough in half and set each piece on a parchment-lined baking sheet. Using your fingers, stretch the dough into a circle or, my preference, a rustic oblong shape. Brush each piece of dough all over with the infused oil (see note). Scatter half the strands of shredded mozzarella over each pizza, leaving some gaps between the pieces. (You don't want the entire pizza covered; the mozzarella will spread.) Sprinkle the Parmesan on. Let the pizzas rest for several minutes, until they've started to puff up slightly, then put into the oven. Bake the pizzas until the crusts are golden and the cheese has melted and gone golden in patches, about 10 to 15 minutes. Remove from the oven.

In a large bowl, combine the salad greens and herbs. Toss the salad with a couple of spoonfuls of the vinaigrette, until just lightly dressed, and divide between the 2 pizzas, sprinkling overtop.

Serve immediately.

SERVES 4 TO 6

This pizza is particularly delicious if you take the cooked garlic from the infused oil and sprinkle it overtop along with the salad. Optional, but lovely.

leek, lemon and potato frittata with goat cheese

8 ounces (250 g) small
potatoes, cut into quarters
or small chunks

1 tablespoon (15 mL) extra
virgin olive oil or vegetable
oil

2 leeks, white and pale green
parts thinly sliced, rinsed
and drained

8 eggs

½ teaspoon (2.5 mL) salt

¼ teaspoon (1 mL) freshly
ground pepper

4 ounces (125 g) goat cheese,
crumbled

zest of 1 lemon

¼ cup (60 mL) parsley,
chopped

Frittatas are easy and multi-purpose. Knowing how to make a basic one is an excellent recipe to have in your repertoire for everything from Sunday brunch to a light but filling dinner. This version uses hearty potatoes and the soft onion flavour of leeks, along with a bristle of lemon zest for freshness. The goat cheese adds richness as well.

Preheat the broiler.

Bring a pot of water to a boil, salt heavily and add the cut potatoes, cooking until just fork tender, then drain.

Meanwhile, set a large ovenproof frying pan over medium heat. Add the oil and warm until shimmering slightly, then add the leeks and sauté until soft and just starting to turn brown in parts. Add the cooked potatoes and stir to distribute evenly so there are chunks of potato and leeks spread around the pan. Reduce the heat to medium-low.

In a bowl, whisk the eggs with salt and pepper. Pour the eggs into the pan and swirl slightly to get the mixture all over the pan to the edges. Using a spatula, lightly push the eggs inward from the edge, letting the uncooked egg fill the space. Continue cooking until the frittata is almost set.

Crumble the goat cheese over the frittata and put it into the oven. Broil until slightly puffed up and golden, 2 to 3 minutes. Remove, then run a spatula around the edge to loosen the frittata, and slide onto a plate. Top with lemon zest and chopped parsley and serve immediately.

SERVES 4 TO 6

chicken with lemon, chorizo and oregano

4 to 6 chicken thighs
  (about 2 pounds [1 kg])
salt
freshly ground pepper
1 lemon
1 tablespoon (15 mL) extra
  virgin olive oil
8 ounces (250 g) dry Spanish
  chorizo, sliced ½ inch (1 cm)
  thick (see note)
8 sprigs fresh oregano,
  divided
1 large shallot, diced
2 cloves garlic, minced
¼ cup (60 mL) chicken stock
1 tablespoon (15 mL) butter
  (optional)

Dry Spanish chorizo
is a hard pork sausage
flavoured with smoked
paprika, which also
gives it a deep brick-
red colour. Although
it comes in both spicy
and sweet versions,
spicy is best for this
recipe. Find it in the deli
department of larger
grocery stores or, often,
at Italian markets.

There's a Spanish influence in this dish, what with spicy chorizo for heat, plus tart lemon and herby oregano adding lots of flavour to the chicken.

Preheat the oven to 425°F (220°C).

Over medium-high heat, warm an ovenproof frying pan large enough to fit the chicken in one layer with some space in-between. Liberally season the chicken thighs with salt and freshly ground pepper.

Slice half the lemon into ⅛-inch (3 mm) rounds, leaving the other half uncut.

Add the oil to the pan and swirl to coat the bottom. When it's hot, add the chicken pieces skin side down. Sauté until cooked about halfway and the skin is golden and has rendered its fat. Spoon off the majority of the oil, leaving a thin layer still coating the pan. Turn over the chicken. Scatter the lemon slices and chorizo into the pan around the chicken thighs, then toss in 6 of the oregano sprigs.

Place the pan in the oven and bake the chicken until completely cooked through, about 10 minutes. (The internal temperature should reach 165°F [74°C].)

Set the pan back on the stove, remove the chicken, chorizo, lemon and oregano to a serving dish, and set aside.

Leaving an oven mitt on one hand to hold the pan, add the shallot and garlic and sauté over medium heat until fragrant and soft, about 1 to 2 minutes. Add the chicken stock, scraping up the lovely, flavourful brown bits on the bottom of the pan. Squeeze in the juice of the remaining half of the lemon. Let reduce slightly. Remove from the heat and add the butter, if using, stirring until it's mixed in completely and the sauce is thicker and glossy. Pour the reduction around the chicken and chorizo, then sprinkle the oregano leaves from the remaining 2 sprigs overtop and serve.

SERVES 4

moroccan stew with preserved lemon

3 tablespoons (45 mL)
  vegetable oil
3 pounds (1.5 kg) chicken
  pieces, skin-on (drumsticks,
  thighs or breasts or a
  combination)
salt
freshly ground pepper
2 yellow onions, peeled and
  sliced in half moons
4 cloves garlic, crushed
2 teaspoons (10 mL) ground
  ginger
1 teaspoon (5 mL) ground
  cinnamon
½ teaspoon (2.5 mL) ground
  cumin
½ teaspoon (2.5 mL) turmeric
½ teaspoon (2.5 mL) saffron
  threads
1½ cups (375 mL) chicken
  stock
2 preserved lemons (see
  notes)
parsley or cilantro, chopped
  (optional)

I ate a lot of things during a week-long trip to Morocco, but, unexpectedly, only two of the tagine stews the country is known for. One was a cinnamon-heavy, thick and hearty chicken version; the other was much lighter, with green beans, artichoke and fresh lemon. This version is a cross between the two. The sauce is full of aromatic spices, but spiked at the end with chopped preserved lemon, which adds a tangy flavour and cuts the richness. No preserved lemons on hand? There is a down-and-dirty quick version (page 201) in the Basics section that I often use for this dish.

Preheat the oven to 350°F (175°C) (see note).

Set a large cast iron pot or deep heavy-bottomed skillet over medium-high heat, add the oil and watch for it to shimmer.

Pat the chicken pieces dry and season liberally with salt and pepper. Add to the heated oil and brown on all sides, taking care not to crowd the pot. (This may be done in batches.) Once browned, remove the chicken to a plate.

Reduce the heat to medium-low and add the onions. Cook, stirring often, until they are soft and golden, about 10 minutes. Add the garlic and cook for another minute or so, until fragrant. Add the spices and sauté with the onions and garlic until fragrant and well mixed, about 2 to 3 minutes. Pour in the stock, scraping up any of the flavourful browned bits left on the bottom of the pot. Return the chicken to the pot and turn up the heat until the sauce just begins to boil, then cover and place in the oven to bake until cooked through, about 30 minutes.

Roughly chop the preserved lemons until the pieces are about ⅛ to ¼ inch big (3 to 6 mm). They don't all have to be the same size; having some pieces slightly bigger and others smaller is nice when mixed in with the stew. When the chicken is cooked, add the preserved lemon, stir well and return the dish to the oven for another 5 minutes. Taste for seasonings, and then sprinkle chopped parsley or cilantro over, if using, and serve.

SERVES 4 TO 6

Find preserved lemons in Middle Eastern and ethnic stores or make your own. (There are 2 recipes, including a quick version that can be made while the stew cooks, in the Basics section on pages 198–201) If using Quick Preserved Lemons, double the recipe to make 2 preserved lemons.

With either quick or regular preserved lemons, there's no need to discard the lemon pulp; just chop it as well and throw in. However, some people like to use just the rind, which is also fine.

Because preserved lemons will have varying levels of salt, wait until after they have been added before tasting to see if more is needed.

Those with a little more time to spare may want to preheat the oven to 300°F (150°C) and cook the chicken for an hour, which makes it even more tender.

lemon chicken

2 large chicken breasts
(about 1 pound [500 g])

2 tablespoons (30 mL)
cornstarch

1 tablespoon (15 mL) sherry or
rice wine

1 tablespoon (15 mL) soy sauce

vegetable or peanut oil for
frying

1 cup (250 mL) tempura
batter, prepared according
to package instructions

1/3 cup (80 mL) chicken stock

1 teaspoon (5 mL) lemon zest

1/4 cup (60 mL) lemon juice

2 tablespoons (30 mL) rice
vinegar

3 tablespoons (45 mL) sugar

1/4 teaspoon (1 mL) salt

1 tablespoon (15 mL)
cornstarch

Going out for Chinese food always means ordering a plate of lemon chicken. That shatter-crisp crust over thin pieces of chicken, all covered in a bright yellow lemon sauce, is my favourite. My version uses tempura batter for a light but crisp crust and a lemon sauce that is bright and tangy without the electric yellow colour.

Using a knife, cut the chicken breasts into 3 pieces on a very sharp angle. Place the chicken between 2 pieces of parchment paper and pound with a meat mallet to get a uniform thickness to each piece.

In a bowl large enough to fit the chicken, mix together the cornstarch, sherry and soy sauce. Add the chicken and let marinate for 1 hour in the fridge.

Add the vegetable oil to a large frying pan or cast iron pot until it is at least 1 inch (2.5 cm) deep. Set over medium-high heat and bring it to 350°F (175°C), checking with a thermometer. When the oil is hot, remove the chicken from the marinade and shake to get any excess off. Dip it in the prepared tempura batter and then fry, 1 or 2 pieces at a time, until golden and cooked through. Remove fried pieces to a paper towel–lined plate.

While the chicken cooks, prepare the sauce. In a small saucepan, mix together the stock, lemon zest and juice, rice vinegar, sugar and salt. Over medium heat, cook the sauce until hot and the sugar has dissolved. Mix the cornstarch with a tablespoon (15 mL) or so of cold water, then add to the lemon sauce and stir until thickened. Remove from heat and cover.

When all the chicken is cooked, place on a platter to serve and drizzle the lemon sauce over it.

SERVES 4

banh mi burgers with spicy lime mayo and pickled carrots

1 egg

4 green onions, thinly sliced

3 cloves garlic, minced

zest of 1 lime

1 tablespoon (15 mL) lime juice

1 tablespoon (15 mL) brown
   sugar

2 teaspoons (10 mL) fish sauce

2 teaspoons (10 mL) chili paste

1 teaspoon (5 mL) minced
   fresh ginger

½ teaspoon (2.5 mL) salt

1 pound (500 g) ground pork

1½ tablespoons (22.5 mL)
   cornstarch

¼ cup (60 mL) panko
   (approximately)

1 tablespoon (15 mL)
   vegetable oil

4 burger buns

Spicy Lime Mayo (recipe
   follows)

Pickled Carrots (recipe
   follows)

fresh basil or cilantro (or
   both)

I have an unabashed, well-publicized, never-ending love for burgers. So, there definitely had to be one in this book. This pork burger is a play on Vietnamese banh mi sandwiches with a mayo I spiked with chili paste and cooling pickled carrots. Friends of mine have debated what the best bun is for the "Big Mi" burger, as it has since been nicknamed. Whether they side with sesame buns or hearty kaisers, all agree the buns should be lightly toasted.

Start by putting together the Spicy Lime Mayo and Pickled Carrots (recipes below), which can be made ahead and refrigerated until you're ready to assemble the burgers.

To make the burgers, in a large bowl whisk together the egg, green onions, garlic, lime zest and juice, brown sugar, fish sauce, chili paste, ginger and salt until well combined. Add the ground pork and mix gently with your hands. (Overworking will lead to tough burgers.) Sprinkle the cornstarch and about half the panko over it, then gently mix again. If the pork mixture is too wet, add the rest of the panko. Divide the mixture evenly into quarters.

Add the oil to a large pan set over medium-high heat. When it starts to shimmer, form the pork mixture into balls, then squish slightly until they're about 1 inch (2.5 cm) thick. Press a dimple into the centre of each—this keeps the patty flat once cooked. Add the patties to the pan and fry until cooked through, flipping once, about 12 minutes total. (An internal temperature probe should read 160°F [71°C].)

Remove to a plate and assemble the burgers. Dollop some of the Spicy Lime Mayo onto the bottom of each bun (or both sides, because a good burger is a messy burger) and then top each one with a patty and some of the drained Pickled Carrots. Add fresh basil or cilantro leaves, if desired, and then the top half of the bun.

SERVES 4

RECIPE CONTINUED ON NEXT PAGE

spicy lime mayo

½ cup (125 mL) mayonnaise (approximately)

3 green onions, thinly sliced

zest of 1 lime

1 tablespoon (15 mL) lime juice

1½ teaspoons (7.5 mL) chili paste (such as sambal oelek)

In a small bowl, mix together all the ingredients. If the mixture seems too thin, add another tablespoon (15 mL) or so of mayonnaise to thicken. Taste for seasonings—adding more chili paste, if desired—and then refrigerate while making the burgers.

pickled carrots

3 tablespoons (45 mL) rice vinegar

3 tablespoons (45 mL) sugar

½ teaspoon (2.5 mL) salt

2 cups (500 mL) julienned carrots (about ½ pound [250 g])

In a bowl large enough to fit the carrots, mix together the vinegar, 2 tablespoons (30 mL) hot water (from the tap is fine), sugar and salt. Stir together until the sugar and salt have dissolved. Add the carrots, mixing them in the pickling liquid. Set aside, stirring occasionally.

These can be made a few hours in advance and refrigerated until you're ready to make the burgers.

citrus-braised pork shoulder tacos

2½ pounds (1.25 kg) boneless pork shoulder

salt

2 jalapeños, stemmed and roughly chopped

4 cloves garlic, roughly chopped

¼ red onion, roughly chopped

juice of 3 limes

juice of 2 lemons

½ cup (125 mL) orange juice

½ cup (125 mL) cider vinegar

2 tablespoons (30 mL) brown sugar

¾ teaspoon (4 mL) freshly ground pepper

½ teaspoon (2.5 mL) allspice

½ teaspoon (2.5 mL) ground cloves

½ teaspoon (2.5 mL) nutmeg

2 tablespoons (30 mL) vegetable oil

1½ cups (375 mL) chicken stock

2 bay leaves

flour or corn tortillas (see note)

Braising pork shoulder in a mixture of spices and lemon and lime juices renders it tender enough to be shredded with a spoon, while the liquid reduces to a sticky-spicy sauce. (It also serves as amazing aromatherapy toward the end of cooking.) I like to shred the meat and mix it completely with the sauce before piling it onto tortillas and topping with Guacamole, fresh Pico de Gallo and my Citrus-Pickled Onions (pages 205 and 202).

Preheat the oven to 350°F (175°C).

Cut the pork shoulder into cubes about 1½ to 2 inches (4 to 5 cm) in size and salt liberally.

In a food processor, combine the jalapeños, garlic, red onion, citrus juices, vinegar, sugar and spices. Purée until the jalapeños, garlic and red onion are completely minced and everything has come together. Set aside.

In a large cast iron pot set over medium-high heat, add the oil and watch for it to shimmer. In batches, add the pork and brown on all sides, taking care not to crowd the pot, which will cause the meat to steam instead of brown. Remove the pork to a plate and continue cooking the pieces until all of them have been browned.

Add the chicken stock to the pot, scraping up all the browned bits left on the bottom. Pour in the spice-juice mixture and the bay leaves and let it all come to a boil. Return the browned pork to the pot, along with any juices that have accumulated on the plate, cover with a lid and place it in the oven. Braise until the meat is tender and the liquid has reduced to a sticky sauce, about 3 hours.

Remove the bay leaves and shred the meat, mixing it with the reduced sauce. Serve with corn or flour tortillas and garnish with Guacamole, Pico de Gallo and Citrus-Pickled Onions (pages 205 and 202).

SERVES 6

I typically use flour tortillas because they are easier to make or find at the grocery store. I like the small-sized ones that fit nicely in your hand even when jammed full of braised pork and toppings. Depending on the size, you'll need between 12 and 16 or so tortillas, but I always err on the side of having more, just in case.

veal scaloppine limone

¼ cup (60 mL) flour

½ teaspoon (2.5 mL) salt

¼ teaspoon (1 mL) freshly ground pepper

1 to 1½ pounds (500 to 750 g) veal scaloppine, pounded to ⅛-inch (3 mm) thickness

1 tablespoon (15 mL) extra virgin olive oil

2 tablespoons (30 mL) butter, divided

⅓ cup (80 mL) dry white wine

1 to 1½ tablespoons (15 to 22.5 mL) lemon juice

2 tablespoons (30 mL) parsley, chopped

This is a very traditional Italian dish that uses cuts of veal pounded incredibly thin and then dredged in flour and fried before lemon is added. The meat is rich but the lemon sauce is the perfect counterpoint. Chicken can easily be substituted for the veal.

On a plate, combine the flour, salt and pepper and stir until thoroughly mixed. Lightly dredge the veal, dusting off the excess.

Heat a large pan over medium-high heat. Once the pan is hot, add the olive oil and 1 tablespoon (15 mL) of the butter. Wait until the butter has melted and starts to foam slightly before adding the veal, ensuring there is space between the scaloppine. Don't crowd the pan; these can be cooked in shifts. Cook until lightly golden, about 2 to 3 minutes, and then turn over to cook the other side. Remove to a plate.

Add the wine to the pan and simmer until it has reduced by half. Add 1 tablespoon (15 mL) of the lemon juice and let reduce further, until slightly thickened. Taste and add up to ½ tablespoon (7.5 mL) more lemon juice if needed. Remove the pan from the heat and add the remaining butter, stirring quickly as it melts. Add the parsley, stir to mix it all together and then pour over the veal to serve.

SERVES 4

bistecca alla fiorentina with arugula-anchovy salad

⅓ cup (80 mL) extra virgin
  olive oil
zest and juice of 1 lemon
5 cloves garlic, minced
1 sprig rosemary, finely
  chopped
1 teaspoon (5 mL) chili flakes
2½ pounds (1.25 kg)
  porterhouse steak, 1¾ to
  2 inches (4.5 to 5 cm) thick
sea salt (see note)
freshly ground pepper
Arugula-Anchovy Salad
  (recipe follows)

When I told friends I was travelling to Italy and a stop in Florence was involved, all agreed that trying bistecca alla fiorentina was a must. The beauty of this steak is in its massive size and how simply it is prepared. My friend Chef Michael Allemeier offered his version of this Italian classic dish, which is best when cooked over a charcoal fire.

In a small bowl, mix together the olive oil, lemon zest, garlic, rosemary and chili flakes. Brush over the steak and refrigerate for 4 to 6 hours.

Remove the steak from the fridge to start bringing it up to room temperature before preparing the charcoal fire or turning on the barbecue.

Build a charcoal fire and set the grill about 4 inches over the coals. The coals should be quite hot—hot enough that you can hold your hand at grill height for only about 4 seconds. (These can also be done on a conventional barbecue. Heat to the same point, when a hand at grill height can be held for only about 4 seconds.)

Place the steak on the grill, letting it sear briefly before reducing the heat by either raising the grill slightly or closing the lower vents. Keep the heat constant and intense, fanning the coals if they look like they are cooling. Grill to desired doneness, turning only once, halfway through cooking. For a 2-inch (5 cm) steak, rare will take about 14 to 16 minutes, medium rare 16 to 20 minutes and medium 20 to 24 minutes, depending on the grill and temperature. (These cook times are for a hot grill at approximately 450°F [230°C]. Thinner steaks will take slightly less time.)

RECIPE CONTINUED ON NEXT PAGE

Sea salt's mild flavour works well to simply enhance the taste of the steak here. Table salt can be substituted, but use a fine hand when adding it.

As the steak cooks, grill a halved lemon alongside to squeeze over before serving. Remove steak from the grill and let rest in a warm place for 5 to 10 minutes. While the steak is resting, assemble the Arugula-Anchovy Salad.

Season the steak well with salt, pepper and a squeeze of the lemon juice. Carve the steak so each person gets both a piece of the tenderloin and striploin. Serve with the salad.

SERVES 2

arugula-anchovy salad

2 cups (500 mL) arugula,
  washed and dried
3 to 5 anchovies
2 cloves garlic, chopped
juice of ½ lemon
⅓ cup (80 mL) extra virgin
  olive oil

Place the arugula in a bowl. Using a mortar and pestle, purée the anchovies and garlic until smooth. Add the lemon juice and mix thoroughly, then slowly whisk in the olive oil. Toss the arugula with the dressing.

lemon-rosemary lamb chops

zest and juice of 1 lemon

2 cloves garlic, minced

1½ tablespoons (22.5 mL) finely chopped rosemary, divided

1 tablespoon (15 mL) extra virgin olive oil

½ teaspoon (2.5 mL) salt

½ teaspoon (2.5 mL) freshly ground pepper

8 lamb loin chops, about 1½ inches (4 cm) thick

zest of 1 lemon, for serving

flaked salt or fleur de sel

There are few flavour combinations I love more than lemon with rosemary (as you can tell from other recipes in this book). Although I have a deep love of lamb with mint sauce, it pairs very well with woodsy rosemary and the bright tang of lemon. This is a simple recipe, but the resulting dish tastes like a lot more effort went in.

In a casserole dish just large enough to fit the chops, stir together the zest and juice of 1 lemon, garlic, 1 tablespoon (15 mL) of rosemary, olive oil, salt and pepper. Add the chops and let them marinate on the counter for 15 to 30 minutes, or for longer in the fridge, turning the chops occasionally.

Set a grill pan over medium-high heat and let it get hot before adding the chops. Cook them for about 6 to 8 minutes, depending on their thickness, turning halfway, until they are cooked to medium rare (or longer, as desired). Remove to a serving platter and sprinkle the remaining rosemary, the zest from the second lemon and a pinch or two of flaked salt over the chops.

SERVES 4

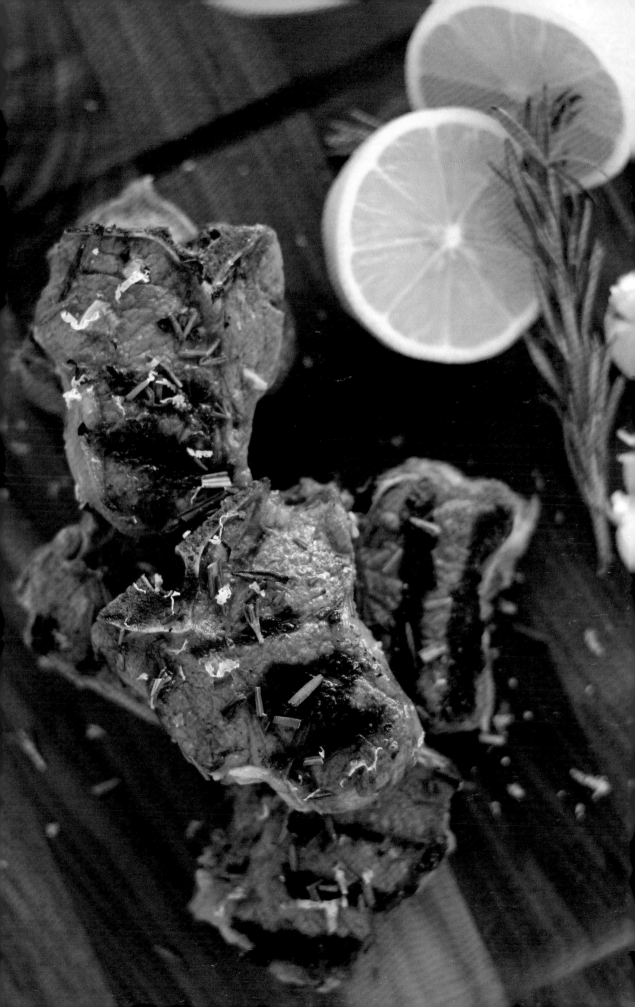

roasted salmon with lemon-herb butter

⅓ cup (80 mL) unsalted
   butter, softened
¼ cup (60 mL) herbs,
   whatever you prefer,
   coarsely chopped
2 teaspoons (10 mL) lemon
   zest
salt
2 pounds (1 kg) salmon fillet
vegetable oil
freshly ground pepper

This salmon takes little more effort than stirring together butter and herbs for a bit and then roasting the fish in the oven. When it's still hot, the herby, lemony butter melts over, creating a simple sauce. Use any herbs, or combination, you like, such as dill, parsley, tarragon or basil. Serve with boiled baby potatoes to sop up all the melted butter.

Preheat the oven to 400°F (200°C).

Mix together the butter, herbs and lemon zest. Add salt to taste (start with about ¼ teaspoon [1 mL] and add more if necessary. The salmon is also seasoned with salt, so if the butter tastes salty enough on its own, it will be fine when melted). Set aside.

In a roasting pan or baking dish, place the salmon skin side down and brush with vegetable oil. Season with salt and pepper. Bake until just cooked, 15 to 20 minutes, depending on the thickness of the fish.

Remove from the oven and slather the butter onto the salmon, letting it melt all over the fish, then serve straight from the baking dish.

SERVES 4 TO 6

grapefruit risotto with seared scallops

1 grapefruit

6 cups (1.5 L) chicken or
  seafood stock

2 tablespoons (30 mL) extra
  virgin olive oil, divided

1 tablespoon (15 mL) butter

1 cup (250 mL) finely diced
  shallots

salt

1½ cups (375 mL) arborio rice

½ cup (125 mL) dry white
  wine

12 large scallops

freshly ground pepper

½ cup (125 mL) grated
  Parmesan

The soft, acidic tang of grapefruit works well to contrast with the creaminess of the risotto in this dish. I also love how the blush-pink colour pops against the off-white and golden-tinged rice and scallops.

With a sharp knife, cut the skin and all the pith off the grapefruit by following the curve of the fruit. Then, over a bowl to catch the juice, cut the segments of the grapefruit between the membranes, releasing the pieces. Squeeze the remaining juice into the bowl and set aside.

In a small saucepan set over medium heat, bring the stock to a gentle simmer. Keep it barely simmering as you prepare the risotto.

In a large saucepan set over medium heat, warm 1 tablespoon (15 mL) of the olive oil and all of the butter until the butter starts to foam slightly. Add the diced shallots, along with a pinch of salt, and gently sauté, stirring occasionally, until softened, 4 to 5 minutes. Do not let the shallots brown. Move the saucepan off the heat slightly if they start to turn golden. Add the rice and stir until each grain is coated, shimmering with the oil and butter, and has gone slightly translucent, about 2 to 3 minutes. Pour in the white wine and stir until most of it is absorbed.

Begin adding the simmering stock, about ½ a cup (125 mL) at a time, stirring often and waiting until most of the liquid has been absorbed before adding more. It should take 3 to 4 minutes for the rice to soak up the liquid between additions. If it's taking a lot less time than that, reduce the heat. If it's taking more, turn up the heat.

RECIPE CONTINUED ON NEXT PAGE

When there is only about a cup (250 mL) or so of stock to go into the risotto, prepare the scallops. Set a heavy-bottomed pan over medium-high heat and add the remaining oil. Pat the scallops dry on both sides and season all over with salt and pepper. When the pan is hot and the oil is shimmering, add the scallops in batches, taking care not to crowd them. Sear until they have a nice golden crust, and then turn them over to sauté the other side. The scallops should still be slightly translucent in the centre. Remove to a plate as the risotto finishes cooking.

Just after the last bit of stock has been added to the risotto, stir in the Parmesan, then the grapefruit segments and juice, mixing gently. Season with salt and pepper to taste.

Divide the risotto among 4 plates. Place 3 scallops atop the risotto on the individual plates and serve.

SERVES 4

baking
& desserts

lime sugar cookies

3¼ cups (810 mL) flour

1 teaspoon (5 mL) baking soda

1 teaspoon (5 mL) salt

½ cup (125 mL) butter, softened

2 cups (500 mL) sugar, plus more for sprinkling

2 tablespoons (30 mL) vegetable oil

zest of 2 limes

¼ cup (60 mL) lime juice

2 eggs

I once bought a cookbook purely for a salad dressing recipe. Later, flipping through it, I discovered a lime sugar cookie recipe that intrigued me (barring a couple of ingredients). A math error led to this version of the cookies that I still make today. They are tangy and sweet with lots of chew and one of my most requested cookies. They are always immediately snapped up wherever I take them.

Preheat the oven to 350°F (175°C) and prepare a cookie sheet by lining it with parchment paper.

In a medium bowl, mix together the flour, baking soda and salt.

In the bowl of a stand mixer fitted with the paddle attachment, beat together the butter, sugar and oil until pale and fluffy, 3 to 4 minutes, scraping down the side as necessary. Add the lime zest and beat again for a minute or two until well mixed and the batter is fragrant. Scrape the side of the bowl and then add the lime juice, mixing on medium speed until incorporated. With the mixer still on medium speed, add the eggs one at a time and beat until well mixed. Add the flour mixture and mix on low speed until just combined.

Using a 1-ounce (30 mL) scoop or soup spoon, portion out the dough onto the prepared cookie sheet, spacing the scoops about 2 inches (5 cm) apart. Squish each one slightly and sprinkle with a pinch or two of sugar.

Bake until just golden at the edges, 8 to 10 minutes. The tops will be slightly crackled, but still puffy and shiny in the centre. They will fall and crack as they cool. Let cool for a few minutes on the cookie sheet and then remove to a cooling rack.

MAKES ABOUT 30 COOKIES

chewy lemon cookies

2¾ cups (685 mL) flour

1 teaspoon (5 mL) baking soda

½ teaspoon (2.5 mL) baking
  powder

½ teaspoon (2.5 mL) salt

1 cup (250 mL) butter,
  softened

1½ cups (375 mL) sugar,
  divided

zest of 1 lemon

1 egg

¼ cup (60 mL) lemon juice

The search for a chewy lemon cookie recipe brings lots of traffic to my blog. It seems I'm not alone in wanting a cookie that has lots of lemon tang with some sweetness and softness. This cookie hits all those notes.

Preheat the oven to 350°F (175°C) and prepare a cookie sheet by lining it with parchment paper.

In a medium bowl, mix together the flour, baking soda, baking powder and salt.

In the bowl of a stand mixer fitted with the paddle attachment, beat together the butter and 1¼ cups (310 mL) sugar until pale and fluffy, scraping down the side as necessary. Beat in the zest until well combined.

With the mixer on medium speed, add the egg, then the lemon juice, beating until incorporated. Add the flour mixture and mix on low speed until just combined.

Using a spoon, scoop out 1-inch (2.5 cm) balls of dough and roll them between your hands to form spheres. Drop into a small bowl of the remaining ¼ cup (60 mL) of sugar and roll gently with your fingertips to coat the dough on all sides.

Space the dough balls about 2 inches (5 cm) apart on the cookie sheet and bake until the edges are cooked but the tops are still puffy, about 8 to 10 minutes. The cookies will be barely golden at the edges and still look ever so slightly uncooked on top. Cool on the cookie sheet for a few minutes, until the tops have fallen and crinkled. Remove to a cooling rack.

MAKES ABOUT 30 COOKIES

grapefruit polenta cookies

1½ cups (375 mL) flour

½ cup (125 mL) finely ground
  cornmeal

½ teaspoon (2.5 mL) salt

¾ cup (185 mL) butter,
  softened

¾ cup (185 mL) sugar

zest of 1 grapefruit

¼ cup (60 mL) grapefruit juice

1 egg

I was making a lemon version of these cookies for a few years before it suddenly occurred to me to try it out with grapefruit. The cornmeal gives these cookies a slight heartiness, a nuttiness and a nice texture, even though they're still soft and chewy in the centre. To try the lemon version, see the note below.

Preheat the oven to 350°F (175°C) and prepare a cookie sheet by lining it with parchment paper.

In a medium bowl, whisk together the flour, cornmeal and salt.

In the bowl of a stand mixer fitted with the paddle attachment, beat together the butter and sugar until pale and fluffy, about 3 to 4 minutes, scraping down the side as necessary. Add the grapefruit zest and beat again for a minute, then add the juice and mix until combined. Add the egg and beat again, then scrape down the bowl. Add the flour-cornmeal mixture and mix on medium-low speed until just combined.

Scoop out the dough in 1-inch (2.5 cm) balls onto the prepared cookie sheet, leaving 2 inches (5 cm) of space between them. Bake until puffed and barely golden at the edges, about 11 minutes. Let cool slightly and remove to a cooling rack.

MAKES ABOUT 20 COOKIES

For a lemon version, use the zest of 1 lemon and 2 tablespoons (30 mL) of juice in place of the grapefruit.

lemon-lavender shortbread

½ cup (125 mL) butter, softened

⅓ cup (80 mL) sugar

zest of 1 lemon

½ teaspoon (2.5 mL) salt

1 teaspoon (5 mL) lavender (see note)

1 cup (250 mL) flour

Lavender is one of those scents that soothes me, and while it may seem strange to see it here in cookie form, it's come to be one of those flavours I really love when it's used right. The first time I tried lavender shortbread, it was a wonder. Lightly floral but rich with butter and sugar, it's not overpowering. Here, I've paired it with bright lemon to add some freshness.

In the bowl of a stand mixer fitted with the paddle attachment, beat together the butter and sugar until pale and fluffy, about 2 to 3 minutes, scraping down the side of the bowl as necessary. Add the lemon zest and beat again until well mixed. Beat in the salt, then reduce the speed and add the lavender. On low speed, add the flour and mix until the dough comes together. It may be a bit crumbly, so don't overmix. Lay out a large piece of plastic wrap on the counter and scoop the dough out onto it. Form the dough into a log about 1½ inches (4 cm) in diameter and wrap tightly, smoothing and rolling it in the plastic to create a uniform shape. Refrigerate until well chilled, up to overnight.

When ready to bake, preheat the oven to 350°F (175°C) and line a baking sheet with parchment paper.

Slice the dough into ¼-inch (6 mm) rounds. The bottom edge of the dough rounds may crumble while slicing; just squish back into place before putting the slices on the cookie sheet. Place on the cookie sheet and bake until just golden, 8 to 10 minutes. Let cool slightly and then remove to a cooling rack.

MAKES 18 TO 20 COOKIES

Culinary lavender is increasingly easy to find in many grocery stores. Look for it in the spice aisle. Specialty cooking stores also often carry it.

lime-pistachio shortbread

½ cup (125 mL) butter,
  softened
⅓ cup (80 mL) sugar
zest of 2 limes
½ teaspoon (2.5 mL) salt
⅓ cup (80 mL) roasted
  pistachios, finely chopped
1 cup (250 mL) flour

As a kid, I remember spying a container of pistachio nuts in my grandmother's pantry and wondering what on earth they were. This was the era when they were all dyed that electric pink colour and everyone's fingers would get stained when they'd eat them. Thankfully, we're well past those dark days and pistachios have returned to their natural green colour. For these cookies, I've paired pistachios with fragrant lime.

In the bowl of a stand mixer fitted with the paddle attachment, beat together the butter and sugar until pale and fluffy, about 2 to 3 minutes, scraping down the side of the bowl as necessary. Add the lime zest and beat again until well mixed. Beat in the salt, then reduce the speed and add the pistachios. On low speed, add the flour and mix until the dough comes together. It may be a bit crumbly, so don't overmix. Lay out a large piece of plastic wrap on the counter and scoop the dough out onto it. Form the dough into a log about 1½ inches (4 cm) in diameter and wrap tightly, smoothing and rolling it in the plastic to create a uniform shape. Refrigerate until well chilled, up to overnight.

When ready to bake, preheat the oven to 350°F (175°C) and line a baking sheet with parchment paper. Slice the dough into ¼-inch (6 mm) rounds. The bottom edge of the dough rounds may crumble while slicing; just squish back into place before putting the slices on the cookie sheet. Place on the cookie sheet and bake until just golden, 8 to 10 minutes. Let cool slightly and then remove to a cooling rack.

MAKES 18 TO 20 COOKIES

ruby red–rosemary tea cakes

CAKE

2 cups (500 mL) flour

1 teaspoon (5 mL) baking
  powder

½ teaspoon (2.5 mL) salt

¼ teaspoon (1 mL) baking
  soda

1 cup (250 mL) butter,
  softened

1 cup (250 mL) sugar

zest of 1 ruby red grapefruit

2 tablespoons (30 mL) fresh
  rosemary, finely chopped

3 tablespoons (45 mL)
  grapefruit juice

2 eggs

⅓ cup (80 mL) buttermilk

SYRUP

¼ cup (60 mL) grapefruit juice

1 tablespoon (15 mL) sugar

one 2- to 3-inch (5 to 8 cm)
  sprig rosemary

GLAZE

1 cup (250 mL) icing sugar

2 tablespoons (30 mL)
  grapefruit juice

pinch salt

I broil grapefruits with rosemary for breakfast sometimes (page 156), which made me think creating a cake that combines those two flavours—the sweet grapefruit flavour of ruby reds and the piney flavour of rosemary—would be a good idea. Adding both to the batter and the soaking syrup poured overtop intensifies the taste of these blush-pink cakes. You'll probably need two grapefruits in total to make the recipe.

Preheat the oven to 350°F (175°C) and prepare 2 loaf pans by buttering them and lining them with parchment paper with a slight overhang, like a sling.

In a medium bowl, mix together the flour, baking powder, salt and baking soda.

In the bowl of a stand mixer fitted with the paddle attachment, beat the butter and sugar until pale and fluffy, 2 to 3 minutes, scraping down the side of the bowl as necessary. Add the grapefruit zest and continue beating for another minute, then add the rosemary, mixing until combined.

With the beaters on low speed to prevent splashing, add the grapefruit juice and mix until it's completely worked in. Return the mixer to medium-high speed and add the eggs, one at a time. Scrape down the side of the bowl after each one. Add the flour mixture and buttermilk in 3 additions, starting with half the flour, then the buttermilk, then the rest of the flour mixture. Mix only until just combined.

Divide the batter between the 2 prepared loaf pans, smoothing the top and rapping the tins on the counter a few times to knock out any air bubbles. Bake until slightly golden and a cake tester comes out clean, about 35 minutes.

While the cakes are baking, prepare the syrup. In a small saucepan, combine the grapefruit juice, sugar and rosemary sprig. Heat over medium-low until the sugar has dissolved and the rosemary has gone a bit soft, about 5 minutes. Set aside to cool.

After the cakes are fully baked, let them cool in the pans for about 10 minutes. Remove the rosemary from the syrup. Using a wooden skewer, poke holes all over the cakes and then gently spoon the syrup over the tops of them. Let them cool completely and then remove from the pans.

Mix the glaze ingredients together and drizzle overtop, letting it set a bit before serving.

MAKES 2 TEA CAKES

lemon loaf cake with glaze

LOAF

1½ cups (375 mL) flour

½ teaspoon (2.5 mL) salt

¼ teaspoon (1 mL) baking powder

¼ teaspoon (1 mL) baking soda

½ cup (125 mL) butter, softened

1 cup (250 mL) sugar

zest of 2 lemons

2 eggs

⅓ cup (80 mL) plain yogurt

1 tablespoon (15 mL) lemon juice

SYRUP

3 tablespoons (45 mL) sugar

3 tablespoons (45 mL) lemon juice

GLAZE

1 cup (250 mL) icing sugar

2 tablespoons (30 mL) lemon juice

pinch salt

You can't have a book about citrus and not include a standard lemon loaf cake. It's a rule. Or I just made it one. This version has three layers of lemon: in the cake itself, in a syrup doused overtop to sink into the cake while still warm and then in a light glaze to finish. This cake will slump a bit in the centre; think of it as the perfect valley for all that glaze.

Preheat the oven to 350°F (175°C) and prepare a loaf pan by buttering it and lining it with parchment paper with a slight overhang, like a sling.

In a medium bowl, mix together the flour, salt, baking powder and baking soda, stirring lightly.

In the bowl of a stand mixer fitted with the paddle attachment, cream the butter and sugar until pale and fluffy, about 3 to 4 minutes, scraping down the side of the bowl as necessary. Add the lemon zest and beat again until it's completely mixed in and slightly fragrant, about 1 minute. Add the eggs, one at a time, scraping down the side of the bowl after each one. In a small bowl, mix together the yogurt and lemon juice.

Add the flour mixture and yogurt in 3 additions, starting with half the flour, then the yogurt, then the rest of the flour mixture. Mix only until just combined.

Pour into the prepared loaf pan, smoothing the top and rapping the tin on the counter a few times to knock out any air bubbles. Bake until slightly golden and a cake tester comes out clean, about 40 to 45 minutes.

As it bakes, prepare the syrup. In a small saucepan, combine the sugar and lemon juice and set over medium-low heat. Cook, stirring occasionally, until the sugar has completely dissolved. Remove from the heat and set aside.

After the loaf has fully baked, let it cool in its pan for about 10 minutes. Using a wooden skewer, poke holes all over the loaf and then gently spoon the syrup overtop. Let it cool completely and then remove from the pan.

Mix the glaze ingredients together and drizzle overtop, letting it set a bit before serving.

MAKES 1 LOAF CAKE

earl grey cupcakes with lemon buttercream

CUPCAKES

¾ cup (185 mL) 2% milk

2 bags Earl Grey tea

1½ cups (375 mL) flour

1½ teaspoons (7.5 mL) baking powder

½ teaspoon (2.5 mL) salt

½ cup (125 mL) butter, softened

1 cup (250 mL) sugar

zest of 1 lemon

2 eggs

BUTTERCREAM

½ cup (125 mL) butter, softened

2 cups (500 mL) icing sugar

¼ teaspoon (1 mL) salt

zest of 1 lemon

2 tablespoons (30 mL) lemon juice (approximately)

I believe I'm the only journalist on the planet who doesn't like coffee. Despite numerous attempts over the years, I'd just rather have a nice cup of tea. I've been drinking it since I was a child and spent the summers visiting my grandparents on one of the Gulf Islands. For breakfast, I'd occasionally have a cup of blackcurrant tea, sweetened with sugar and spiked with a slice of lemon. These days, I still like lemon and sugar in my tea, but I usually drink Earl Grey, which is fragrant with citrus-scented bergamot. These cupcakes are an homage to that love of combining tea and lemon.

Preheat the oven to 350°F (175°C). Lightly grease a muffin tin or line with paper liners.

In a small saucepan set over medium heat, scald the milk, then remove from the heat and add the 2 tea bags. Let them steep, and cool to room temperature, then remove the tea bags, squeezing out any milk.

In a medium bowl, mix together the flour, baking powder and salt until well combined.

In the bowl of a stand mixer fitted with the paddle attachment, cream the butter and the sugar until pale and fluffy, about 3 to 4 minutes, scraping the side of the bowl as necessary. Beat in the lemon zest. Add the eggs, one at a time, making sure each is thoroughly mixed in before adding the next one, scraping the side of the bowl each time.

With the mixer on low speed, add half of the flour mixture and beat until nearly combined. Add the tea-steeped milk and mix until just combined, then add the rest of the flour mixture. Stir until just combined.

Divide the cupcake batter between the 12 cups, filling each about two-thirds full. Bake until barely golden and a cake tester comes out clean, about 20 to 25 minutes. Let cool before frosting.

In the bowl of a stand mixer fitted with the paddle attachment, beat the butter and icing sugar until pale and fluffy, about 3 to 4 minutes. Add the salt, lemon zest and juice and beat again until smooth. Taste for flavour, adding more lemon juice if desired. (If the icing is too thick, add a splash of milk or a bit more lemon juice; if it's too thin, beat in more icing sugar.) Spread over the cooled cupcakes.

MAKES 12 CUPCAKES

grandma madelon's baked lemon pudding cake

1½ cups (375 mL) sugar,
  divided

½ cup (125 mL) flour

½ teaspoon (2.5 mL) baking
  powder

¼ teaspoon (1 mL) salt

3 eggs, separated

zest of 1 lemon (or 2, if you
  like it zingy)

¼ cup (60 mL) lemon juice

1½ cups (375 mL) 2% milk

2 tablespoons (30 mL) melted
  butter

Recipes handed down through the generations are the best. I love how those typed out or carefully handwritten, then spattered and stained from use over the years, are little pieces of culinary history. This recipe from Julie Van Rosendaal's grandmother for a baked lemon cake is just one of those. And the recipe is like alchemy; it comes out warm and golden, with a cake hiding soft and lemony pudding underneath.

Preheat the oven to 375°F (190°C).

In a large bowl, stir together 1 cup (250 mL) of the sugar with the flour, baking powder and salt.

In a small bowl, stir together the egg yolks, lemon zest, lemon juice, milk and butter. Add to the dry ingredients, mixing just until combined.

In a clean glass or stainless steel bowl, beat the egg whites until soft peaks form, gradually adding the remaining ½ cup (125 mL) sugar, beating constantly until the mixture stands in stiff peaks. Gently fold into the lemon batter, then scrape into a buttered 8-inch (20 cm) square baking dish.

Set the baking dish into a larger dish, and fill that one up with enough water to reach halfway up the sides of the smaller dish. Bake for 45 minutes, until golden and springy to the touch. Serve warm or cold.

SERVES 8

flourless chocolate-lime cake

¾ cup (185 mL) butter
¼ cup (60 mL) cocoa
8 ounces (250 g) dark
   chocolate, 70% cocoa,
   chopped
6 eggs
1 cup (250 mL) sugar
¼ teaspoon (1 mL) salt
zest and juice of 1 lime
zest of 1 lime, for serving

The first time I tried the combination of lime and chocolate was when I made a cheesecake from Nigella Lawson. They seemed a peculiar match, but it totally worked. Later, I stumbled onto a brownie recipe that also brought together rich chocolate and tangy lime; it worked just as well. I knew I wanted something that mingled these two flavours together as a dessert—something a bit fancier than a brownie, less creamy than a cheesecake. What I came up with was a flourless chocolate cake, intensely rich and darkly chocolate, not overly sweet, and bristling with lime zest and juice. Zesting over another lime just before serving adds a nice touch of green and enhances the flavour.

Preheat the oven to 350°F (175°C) and prepare a 9-inch (23 cm) springform pan by buttering the bottom and sides.

In a small saucepan set over medium-low heat, melt the butter and stir in the cocoa. Add the chopped chocolate and stir until it is completely melted. Set aside.

In a large bowl, whisk together the eggs, sugar and salt until the mixture doesn't feel gritty and the eggs have gone pale and thick. Add the zest and juice of 1 lime and whisk again until thoroughly combined. Pour in the melted chocolate mixture and stir until well mixed.

Pour into the prepared springform pan and bake until the top appears dry and the centre barely jiggles, about 40 to 45 minutes. Let cool for 1 hour, then run a knife around the cake before releasing the springform. Cool completely.

Just before serving, zest the second lime all over the top of the cake. Serve in thin wedges.

MAKES 1 CAKE

rosemary, pine nut and fleur de sel shortbread lemon bars

BASE

¾ cup (185 mL) butter,
softened

½ cup (125 mL) sugar

¾ teaspoon (4 mL) fleur de sel
(see notes)

½ cup (125 mL) pine nuts,
toasted, cooled and
chopped

1 tablespoon (15 mL) fresh
rosemary, chopped

1½ cups (375 mL) flour

FILLING

2 eggs

1 cup (250 mL) sugar

zest of 2 lemons

½ cup (125 mL) lemon juice

2 tablespoons (30 mL)
whipping cream

2 tablespoons (30 mL) flour

¼ teaspoon (1 mL) salt

icing sugar for dusting
(optional)

One of my favourite cookies is a shortbread from Heidi Swanson of the blog *101 Cookbooks* that brings together lemon zest, rich pine nuts and that lovely, woodsy flavour of rosemary. One of my favourite bars is the lemon bar, of course. I thought bringing together those two things would make for a fantastic combination and I'm glad I thought it was worth the attempt. Finding the right balance between the shortbread base and lemon topping took a few tries, but this version is just right.

Butter an 8-inch (20 cm) square pan and line with parchment paper, letting a few inches hang over each side, like a sling.

In the bowl of a stand mixer fitted with the paddle attachment, beat together the butter and sugar until pale and fluffy, 2 to 3 minutes, scraping down the side as necessary. Add the salt and beat again. Add the pine nuts and rosemary and mix until well incorporated. Add the flour and mix again on low speed until just combined, scraping the side to ensure all the flour is incorporated.

Scoop into the prepared pan and use your fingers to press into an even layer. Chill in the fridge for 30 minutes.

Preheat the oven to 350°F (175°C). When the shortbread base has chilled, place it in the oven and bake until just golden and set, about 20 to 25 minutes.

While it bakes, make the filling. Whisk the eggs and sugar until well combined, then add the lemon zest, juice and whipping cream. Beat well until smooth, then add the flour and salt. Gently stir until just mixed and no dry flour can be seen.

Once the crust has baked, gently pour the lemon filling overtop and return it to the oven. Bake until the filling has set and is just turning golden, about 22 to 25 minutes. (It should barely jiggle in the centre.) Let cool completely.

Dust with icing sugar, if desired. Run a knife along the edges touching the pan and use the parchment paper sling to lift it out. Cut into bars.

MAKES ABOUT 25 BARS, DEPENDING ON HOW LARGE
A BAR YOU WANT

I normally don't fuss over fancy cooking salts, but in this case I like using fleur de sel, which has larger crystals and a softer taste than table salt. Fleur de sel ("flower of salt" in French) is harvested from evaporating sea water. It is an excellent finishing salt for sprinkling over cooked meats and vegetables. You can find it in most major grocery stores, as well as gourmet stores.

You can substitute ½ teaspoon (2.5 mL) table salt.

lemon bars

BASE

½ cup (125 mL) butter,
  softened
¼ cup (60 mL) sugar
pinch salt
1 cup (250 mL) flour

FILLING

2 eggs
1 egg yolk
1 cup (250 mL) sugar
zest of 2 lemons
⅓ cup (80 mL) lemon juice
2 tablespoons (30 mL) flour
¼ teaspoon (1 mL) baking
  powder
¼ teaspoon (1 mL) salt
icing sugar for dusting
  (optional)

A classic for a reason, I find lemon bars are often the first to get snatched up from a buffet table. This version makes an equally good lime bar by simply substituting lime juice and zest (see note).

Butter an 8-inch (20 cm) square pan and line with parchment paper, letting a few inches hang over each side, like a sling.

In the bowl of a stand mixer fitted with the paddle attachment, beat together the butter and sugar until pale and fluffy, 2 to 3 minutes, scraping down the side as necessary. Add the salt and beat again. Add the flour and mix again on low speed until just combined, scraping the side to ensure all the flour is incorporated. Add to the prepared pan and use your fingers to press into an even layer. Chill in the fridge for 30 minutes.

Preheat the oven to 350°F (175°C). When the shortbread base has chilled, place it in the oven and bake until just golden and set, about 20 to 25 minutes.

While it bakes, make the filling. Whisk together the eggs, yolk and sugar until well combined, then add the lemon zest and juice. Beat well until smooth, then add the flour, baking powder and salt. Gently whisk until just mixed and no dry flour can be seen.

Once the crust has baked, gently pour the lemon filling overtop and return it to the oven. Bake until the filling has set and is just turning golden, about 20 to 25 minutes. (It should barely jiggle in the centre.) Let cool completely.

Dust with icing sugar, if desired. Run a knife along the edges touching the pan and use the parchment paper sling to lift it out. Cut into bars.

MAKES ABOUT 25 BARS, DEPENDING ON HOW LARGE A
BAR YOU WANT

To make Lime Bars, substitute the zest of 3 limes and ⅓ cup (80 mL) lime juice in place of the lemon zest and juice.

tarte au citron

PASTRY

1 cup (250 mL) flour

3 tablespoons (45 mL) sugar

¼ teaspoon (1 mL) salt

½ cup (125 mL) cold butter,
cut into cubes

1 egg yolk

2 tablespoons (30 mL)
whipping cream
(approximately)

FILLING

4 eggs

4 egg yolks

1 cup (250 mL) sugar

zest of 2 lemons

¾ cup (185 mL) lemon juice,
strained

10 tablespoons (150 mL)
butter, cubed

½ teaspoon (2.5 mL) salt

icing sugar for dusting
(optional)

The quintessential French dessert, this tart takes a sweetened and enriched pie crust, bakes it until golden and then fills it with a rich, thick lemon curd. Unlike a lemon meringue pie, there is no adornment with meringue or whipped cream, though I do like to dust with a bit of icing sugar before serving.

In a large bowl, mix together the flour, sugar and salt. Scatter the cubes of butter over and work into the flour using a pastry cutter, 2 knives or your fingertips until it looks like coarse oatmeal, with some pieces the size of peas and others smaller. Beat together the egg yolk and whipping cream in a small bowl and sprinkle over the flour-butter mixture. Toss with a fork until clumps begin to form. Gather the clumps together and press into a ball. If there is still a lot of dry flour, drizzle another tablespoon or so of cream over. The dough should hold together when pinched, but should not be sticky. Pat the pastry into a ball and then flatten slightly. Wrap in plastic and refrigerate until chilled, at least 2 to 3 hours but up to overnight.

When you're ready to make the tart, preheat the oven to 400°F (200°C).

On a lightly floured surface, roll out the pastry to about ¼ inch (6 mm) thick, with enough to form a 1-inch (2.5 cm) overhang in a 9-inch (23 cm) tart tin with a removable bottom. Gently lay the pastry in the tart tin and press into the edge, being careful not to stretch it. Trim the edges with a knife or run a rolling pin over the top of the tart tin to cut the excess off. Prick the pastry with a fork and then line with parchment paper or foil and fill with pie weights or dried beans. Bake the pastry for about 15 to 20 minutes, until it's just starting to turn golden along the edges. Remove the pie weights or beans and continue baking until completely golden, about 10 more minutes.

Prepare the filling. In a double boiler or a metal bowl set over a pot of simmering water, combine the eggs, yolks, sugar and lemon zest and juice. Whisk constantly until the mixture thickens and reaches 160°F (71°C) on a thermometer. Turn off the heat and add the butter a couple of cubes at a time, whisking them in and only adding the next few once the pieces before have been worked into the curd. Stir in the salt. Pour through a fine-mesh sieve into the baked crust and smooth to create an even top. Refrigerate until the curd has set, about 4 hours or overnight.

Dust with icing sugar, if desired, before serving.

MAKES 1 TART

key lime pie

FILLING

4 egg yolks

2 teaspoons (10 mL) lime zest

½ cup (125 mL) lime juice (see note)

one 14-ounce (398 mL) can sweetened condensed milk

CRUST

15 graham crackers, crushed

2 tablespoons (30 mL) sugar

½ cup (125 mL) butter, melted

WHIPPED CREAM (OPTIONAL)

1 cup (250 mL) whipping cream

2 tablespoons (30 mL) sugar

Little key limes have a less sharp flavour than their bigger cousins, but both work in this pie that originated in the Florida Keys (Although the purist in me prefers it made with real key limes.) In the muggy heat of the Keys and the tropical islands around them, this pie grew from a desire for dessert made from ingredients that didn't require refrigeration. Although untraditional, I do like a dollop of whipped cream on top.

Preheat the oven to 350°F (175°C).

In the bowl of a stand mixer fitted with the paddle attachment, beat the egg yolks until they are pale yellow and thickened. Add the zest and beat again. Add the lime juice and condensed milk, then thoroughly beat on medium speed until well mixed. Let the filling sit for about 30 minutes to thicken further.

Blitz the graham crackers in a food processor until they just begin to become crumbs. Add the sugar, then turn on the processor and slowly pour in the melted butter. Press the mixture evenly into a 9-inch (23 cm) pie dish or tart pan, pushing up the sides. Bake until the pie shell is slightly golden, about 12 to 15 minutes.

Pour the lime filling into the pie shell and bake until the filling is set, about 15 minutes. The centre should jiggle slightly when the pan is shaken. Remove from the oven and allow to cool to room temperature before refrigerating. Chill for 3 hours or longer before serving.

Serve with sweetened whipped cream, if desired. For the whipped cream, add the cream to the bowl of a stand mixer fitted with the whisk attachment and whip on medium speed until soft peaks form. Sprinkle the sugar over the cream and beat again. Dollop over the centre of the pie and spread to nearly the edge, or serve on the side.

MAKES 1 PIE

Key limes are often available at grocery stores. You'll need between 12 and 16 (and a lot of patience) to get enough juice, but the extra effort is worth it.

lemon meringue pie

PASTRY

2 cups (500 mL) flour

1 teaspoon (5 mL) salt

⅓ cup (80 mL) butter, cold and cubed

⅓ cup (80 mL) shortening, cold and cubed

¼ cup (60 mL) ice water (approximately)

¼ cup (60 mL) vodka, cold

1 egg white, whisked until lightly frothy

FILLING

1¼ cups (310 mL) sugar

⅓ cup (80 mL) cornstarch

1¼ cups (310 mL) water

5 egg yolks

zest of 1 lemon

½ cup (125 mL) lemon juice

¼ teaspoon (1 mL) salt

3 tablespoons (45 mL) butter, cubed

MERINGUE

4 egg whites

¾ cup (185 mL) sugar

2 tablespoons (30 mL) cornstarch

A solid crust, a thick and tart lemony filling and a cloud-like meringue topping with peaks turned a dark shade of gold: These are the elements that make a good lemon meringue pie. Too often, to my disappointment, the meringue on this classic pie is an insipid blob of egg whites with no flavour. I wanted a topping that was more like a pavlova, with some substance and a bit of a crust to the outer, barely browned edge, but pillowy soft below—a sweet cloud against the robust yet silky lemon filling.

In a large bowl, stir together the flour and salt. Add the cubes of cold butter and shortening and work into the flour with a pastry cutter or 2 knives until it looks like coarse oatmeal, with some pieces the size of peas and others smaller. Stir together ¼ cup (60 mL) ice water and vodka in a small bowl and then sprinkle half over the flour mixture. Lightly gather together the dampened flour to one side of the bowl, pressing it together to form a ball. Sprinkle the rest of the water mixture over the remaining dry flour and pull it together. (If there is still a lot of dry flour and the mixture won't form a ball when pressed together, add another tablespoon [15 mL] or so of ice water.) Pat the pastry into a ball and then flatten slightly. Wrap in plastic and refrigerate until chilled, about 30 minutes. (This can be done ahead, up to overnight.)

Preheat the oven to 400°F (200°C).

On a lightly floured work surface, roll the pastry out to a bit under ¼ inch (6 mm) thick, with enough to form a 1-inch (2.5 cm) overhang in a 9-inch (23 cm) pie plate. Press the pastry into the pie plate, trim and fold the overhang under, then flute the edges or crimp with the tines of a fork. Prick the pastry with a fork and line with parchment paper or foil and fill with pie weights or dried beans. Bake for 15 minutes, then remove the pie weights or beans and bake for another 8 to 10 minutes, until just golden. Remove from the oven and immediately brush the lightly beaten egg white all over the baked crust. (The leftover yolk will go into the filling.)

Reduce the oven to 350°F (175°C).

In a medium saucepan, whisk together the sugar and cornstarch and then add the 1¼ cups (310 mL) water. Add the egg yolks, lemon zest and juice and salt, whisking again until well combined.

RECIPE CONTINUED ON NEXT PAGE

Place the saucepan over medium heat and cook, whisking nearly constantly, until the mixture is thick and starting to bubble. Remove from the heat and add the butter, whisking until it's completely mixed into the filling. Pour into the crust.

In the bowl of a stand mixer fitted with the whisk attachment, beat the egg whites to soft peaks, then add half the sugar and all the cornstarch, beating again until the whites hold stiff peaks. Beat in the rest of the sugar.

Dollop large spoonfuls of meringue onto the still-hot lemon filling, starting at the crust—making sure it adheres to it—and working inward. Using the back of a spoon, swoop the meringue into curls and valleys. Bake the pie until the meringue has started to turn slightly golden in parts, with the peaks a darker gold, about 15 minutes. (Some of the valleys will remain white, which is fine.)

Let the pie cool for about an hour and a half before serving.

MAKES 1 PIE

breakfasts

broiled grapefruit

1 grapefruit
1 tablespoon (15 mL) brown
  sugar
pinch salt

Broiled grapefruit comes across as some sort of stereotypical 1970s breakfast dish—think of those ones with half a maraschino cherry in the centre—but I still love this. The brown sugar gives it a deeper flavour, while the pinch of salt keeps it from being cloyingly sweet. (See note for a variation.)

Adjust the oven rack so it sits on the top rung, then turn on the broiler.

Slice the grapefruit in half and set the halves in an ovenproof dish. Sprinkle each half with half of the brown sugar and then scatter a pinch of salt over the tops.

Broil until the sugar is bubbling and golden, 3 to 5 minutes. Spoon on top any syrup that has spilled over while broiling, if desired.

SERVES 1

This is also great with a bit of coarsely chopped rosemary. Mix with the brown sugar before sprinkling over the cut grapefruit halves and then continue with the rest of the recipe.

fruit salad with lime and mint

¼ cup (60 mL) sugar

6 tablespoons (90 mL) mint
   leaves, coarsely chopped,
   divided

zest and juice of 1 lime

10 cups (2.5 L) fruit, cut into
   bite-sized pieces

zest of 1 lime, for serving

Fruit needs little adornment, so it's a bit cheeky to call for a fruit salad to be topped with a simple syrup infusion. Then again, topping fruit with this "dressing" of mint, lime and sugar only enhances fruit's natural beauty. Use whatever fruit—strawberries, melon, grapefruits, apples, pineapple—is in season or desired.

In a small saucepan set over medium heat, warm the sugar and ½ cup (125 mL) water until the sugar has dissolved. Remove from the heat and stir in 4 tablespoons (60 mL) of the mint. Let steep for a couple of minutes and then add the lime zest and juice. Let cool and then strain out the mint leaves.

When ready to serve, add all the fruit to a large bowl and pour some of the lime-mint syrup over. Toss lightly, adding more of the syrup as necessary. Add the remaining chopped mint, zest the second lime overtop and toss again.

Divide into small bowls or serve directly from the large one.

SERVES 4 TO 6

crêpes with lemon **and** sugar

3 eggs

2 cups (500 mL) milk

1 cup (250 mL) flour

¼ cup (60 mL) melted butter,
   plus more for the pan

pinch salt

¼ to ½ cup (60 to 125 mL)
   sugar

2 to 3 lemons, cut into 6 or
   8 wedges each

Long before all those crêpe kiosks and restaurants popped up, these thin French pancakes were a weekend treat when I was growing up. It wasn't until years later that I found out crêpes can be stuffed with myriad sweet and savoury fillings; for me, it was always about a squeeze of lemon and a sprinkling of sugar. It still is. This recipe is the same one my mum used all those weekend mornings.

In a blender or food processor, combine the eggs, milk, flour, melted butter and salt and pulse for 10 to 20 seconds until a thin batter forms, about the same consistency as whipping cream. Add up to another ¼ cup (60 mL) flour, about a tablespoon (15 mL) at a time, if necessary. Refrigerate for an hour or up to overnight.

When ready to cook, heat a large non-stick pan over medium until a bit of water sprinkled on it sizzles lightly. Add a bit of butter to coat the bottom of the pan and then pour in ¼ to ⅓ cup (60 to 80 mL) of the batter, swirling the pan so it spreads evenly. Cook until the underside of the crêpe is golden, the top looks almost dry and the edges are curling up, about 1 to 2 minutes. Using a spatula, loosen the edge of the crêpe and quickly flip with your fingers. Cook for about 30 seconds more and remove to a plate.

Sprinkle each crêpe with a spoonful or two of sugar and then squeeze 1 or 2 lemon wedges overtop, depending on how sweet or tart you want it. Fold in half and then half again to make a triangle, or roll into a log.

MAKES 10 TO 12 CRÊPES

lemon soufflé pancakes with macerated strawberries

4 eggs, separated
1 cup (250 mL) ricotta
3 tablespoons (45 mL) sugar
zest of 1 lemon
juice of ½ lemon
½ teaspoon (2.5 mL) salt
½ cup (125 mL) flour
Macerated Strawberries
  (recipe follows)

These little pancakes are like cousins to the soufflé they're named after. Light, fluffy and full of lemon flavour, they only need to be adorned with some slightly sweetened strawberries, which you can make ahead and set aside in the fridge until the pancakes are ready. Ricotta from the store simplifies this recipe, but you can also make your own using the recipe (page 206) in the Basics section.

Heat a pan or griddle over medium heat.

In a medium bowl, whisk together the egg yolks, ricotta, sugar, lemon zest and juice and salt. Stir in the flour.

Using a mixer, whip the egg whites until they hold medium peaks—the mixture will stand up on the beaters or whisk but the tip will curl slightly over. Take about one-third of the beaten whites and fold into the ricotta mixture. Add the rest of the whites and gently fold them in with a spatula, scooping lightly from the bottom and folding over until the batter is just mixed.

With the pan hot, add a bit of butter to coat the surface, letting it bubble up a bit. Using a ¼-cup (60 mL) measuring cup, ladle the batter into the pan. Let the pancakes fry until they're cooked and slightly golden underneath, 2 to 3 minutes. Flip. Let cook another minute or two. Remove to a plate and keep warm.

Serve with Macerated Strawberries spooned overtop.

MAKES ABOUT 12 TO 16 PANCAKES

macerated strawberries

1 pint (500 mL) strawberries
1 to 2 tablespoons (15 to
  30 mL) sugar

Hull and dice the strawberries. Add the sugar—more for tart strawberries, less when they're perfectly in season—and stir together. Refrigerate until the pancakes are cooked.

sour cream blackberry-lime muffins

2 cups (500 mL) flour
½ cup (125 mL) sugar
1 teaspoon (5 mL) baking
  powder
1 teaspoon (5 mL) baking soda
½ teaspoon (2.5 mL) salt
zest of 2 limes
1 egg
1¼ cups (310 mL) sour cream
½ cup (125 mL) vegetable oil
juice of 1 lime
1½ cups (375 mL) blackberries,
  fresh or frozen

I love the look of these muffins, the bright green flecks of lime zest against the deeply purple berries. But the flavour is even better. Aromatic lime perfumes the muffins, while the blackberries give nice sweet bursts. You can tell muffins are done when the tops are springy to the touch.

Preheat the oven to 350°F (175°C). Lightly grease a muffin tin or line with paper liners.

In a large bowl, whisk together the flour, sugar, baking powder, baking soda, salt and lime zest. In a separate bowl, whisk together the egg, sour cream, oil and lime juice. Add the wet ingredients to the dry and gently fold until just mixed; it shouldn't need more than 20 stirs to come together. Stirring more is what makes a muffin tough. Add in the berries, taking care to stir the mixture as little as possible.

Divide the batter between the 12 muffin cups. Bake for 20 to 24 minutes, until a tester comes out clean.

MAKES 12 MUFFINS

lemon-ricotta muffins

1 cup (250 mL) flour

6 tablespoons (90 mL) sugar

2 teaspoons (10 mL) baking powder

¼ teaspoon (1 mL) salt

zest and juice of 1 lemon, divided

1¼ cup (310 mL) ricotta

2 eggs, lightly beaten

⅓ cup (80 mL) vegetable oil

Ricotta makes these muffins nice and light and the lemon gives them a sunny taste. But they are equally good when made with the zest and juice of two limes. The trick to keeping muffins from being dense is to stir them as little as possible. It shouldn't take more than 20 stirs to combine the wet and dry ingredients. Most of the time I just use ricotta from the store to make these muffins, but they're equally good with the homemade stuff. Find that recipe (page 206) in the Basics section.

Preheat the oven to 350°F (175°C). Lightly grease a muffin tin or line with paper liners.

In a large bowl, whisk together the flour, sugar, baking powder, salt and lemon zest. In a separate bowl, whisk together the ricotta, lemon juice, eggs and vegetable oil. Add the wet ingredients to the dry and gently fold until just mixed.

Divide the batter between the 12 muffin cups. Bake for 18 to 22 minutes, until a tester comes out clean.

MAKES 12 MUFFINS

meyer lemon coffeecake muffins

STREUSEL

¼ cup (60 mL) packed brown
  sugar
2 tablespoons (30 mL) sugar
¼ teaspoon (1 mL) salt
¼ cup (60 mL) butter, melted
½ to ⅔ cup (125 to 160 mL)
  flour

CAKE

1 Meyer lemon
1 cup (250 mL) flour
½ teaspoon (2.5 mL) baking
  powder
¼ teaspoon (1 mL) baking
  soda
¼ teaspoon (1 mL) salt
¼ cup (60 mL) butter
½ cup (125 mL) sugar
1 egg
½ cup (125 mL) sour cream
Glaze (optional) (recipe
  follows)

I have strong feelings about the difference between muffins and cupcakes. My argument is any time you're creaming butter and sugar (and, particularly, if there is a lot of sugar), you're pretty much in cake territory. So, with that caveat, I present these so-called muffins (though I did put the word "cake" in the title, so that absolves me of some guilt). Mostly, I use the term "muffin" to indicate their shape and size. Years ago, I saw a Meyer lemon coffeecake from Martha Stewart that used whole slices of the lemons layered in the centre. I wanted to do something similar but didn't want to tackle a massive cake. These meet somewhere in the middle.

Start by making the streusel. Mix together the sugars and the salt, then pour the melted butter over and stir. Add ½ cup (125 mL) of the flour and mix with a fork until it forms clumps of all sizes and the mixture appears dry. If it still seems too wet, add the rest of the flour. Refrigerate until ready to use.

Preheat the oven to 350°F (175°C). Lightly grease a muffin tin or line with paper liners.

Using a mandoline or sharp knife, slice the Meyer lemon as thinly as possible, remove the seeds and then coarsely chop the slices.

In a medium bowl, combine the flour, baking powder, baking soda and salt. Whisk to combine.

In the bowl of a stand mixer fitted with the paddle attachment, cream the butter and sugar until pale and fluffy, about 3 to 4 minutes. Add the egg and beat until thoroughly mixed, scraping down the side of the bowl as necessary. Add the flour mixture and sour cream in 3 parts, starting with half the flour mixture, followed by the sour cream and then the rest of the flour. Mix until just combined.

RECIPE CONTINUED ON NEXT PAGE

Portion out half the batter into the muffin cups, then top each with a pinch or two of the chopped Meyer lemon slices, dividing all of the lemon evenly between the muffins. Top with the rest of the batter, hiding the lemon bits. The cups should be only about three-quarters full. Don't overfill.

Sprinkle the streusel over the muffins. Bake until just golden and a cake tester comes out clean, about 20 to 25 minutes. Let cool.

If desired, drizzle with glaze.

MAKES 12 MUFFINS

glaze

1 cup (250 mL) icing sugar
juice of 1 Meyer lemon
pinch salt

Combine the ingredients in a small bowl and stir until well mixed. If the glaze seems too thin, add a bit more icing sugar. Drizzle over the baked and slightly cooled muffins.

grapefruit-ginger scones

2 cups (500 mL) flour
⅓ cup (80 mL) sugar
1 tablespoon (15 mL) baking
   powder
¼ teaspoon (1 mL) ground
   ginger
¼ teaspoon (1 mL) salt
zest of 1 grapefruit
½ cup (125 mL) crystallized
   ginger, chopped
½ cup (125 mL) butter, frozen
1 egg
¾ cup (185 mL) whipping
   cream (approximately)
2 tablespoons (30 mL)
   grapefruit juice
Glaze (optional) (recipe
   follows)

I always had problems with scones until I learned the trick of grating frozen butter into the mixture. Now I keep a block of butter in my freezer at all times for last-minute scone cravings. In this version, I've used crystallized ginger and grapefruit for a spicy, tangy, sweet scone. I've included an optional glaze for drizzling over to make them a little more decadent.

Preheat the oven to 425°F (220°C) and line a baking sheet with parchment paper.

In a large bowl, add the flour, sugar, baking powder, ground ginger, salt, grapefruit zest and chopped crystallized ginger, using a fork or whisk to mix them together well. Grate in the frozen butter and lightly toss with the flour mixture, using your fingertips, until the butter curls are well distributed.

In a small bowl, whisk together the egg, whipping cream and grapefruit juice. Pour into the flour mixture, using a spatula to mix. If the mixture seems too dry, add another tablespoon (15 mL) or so of cream. You don't want it too wet, but you don't want to overmix to get it to come together either.

On a clean counter, pat the dough out into a rough square and cut into 9 pieces by slicing in thirds vertically and horizontally. (Or, to make wedge-shaped scones, pat into a circle and cut into 6.) Place on the prepared baking sheet, spacing them about an inch (2.5 cm) apart. Bake until golden, about 15 to 18 minutes.

If desired, drizzle with glaze.

MAKES 6 TO 9 SCONES

glaze

½ cup (125 mL) icing sugar
1 tablespoon (15 mL)
   grapefruit juice
pinch salt

In a small bowl, mix together the icing sugar, juice and salt. Drizzle over the cooled scones.

glazed lemon-raspberry drop scones

2 cups (500 mL) flour
¼ cup (60 mL) sugar
1 tablespoon (15 mL) baking
  powder
½ teaspoon (2.5 mL) salt
zest of 1 lemon
1¼ cups (310 mL) whipping
  cream (approximately)
1 tablespoon (15 mL) lemon
  juice
1 cup (250 mL) raspberries

GLAZE
1 cup (250 mL) icing sugar
2 tablespoons (30 mL) lemon
  juice
pinch salt
milk or whipping cream to
  thin

Cream scones take butter out of the equation, making them even easier—and, therefore, maybe a bit more dangerous—to make. These are summery scones, flavoured with lemon and punctuated with bright red raspberries. A tangy and sweet glaze drizzled overtop makes these a bit more lavish than a standard scone.

Preheat the oven to 400°F (200°C) and line a baking sheet with parchment paper.

In a large bowl, add the flour, sugar, baking powder, salt and zest, using a fork or whisk to mix them together. Make a well in the centre and pour in the whipping cream and lemon juice. Stir together with a spatula to make a shaggy dough, adding up to an additional ¼ cup (60 mL) cream if necessary. Stir in the raspberries. Some of them will get squished, creating lovely pink streaks, which is totally fine.

Using a large spoon, scoop the dough into mounds on the prepared baking sheet, spacing them about an inch (2.5 cm) or so apart. I like to make 8 large scones, but you can make slightly smaller ones to get more of them out of the dough. Just make sure to decrease the baking time if you do.

Bake the scones until golden-tinged, about 15 minutes. Let them cool.

To make the glaze, mix together the icing sugar, lemon juice and salt in a small bowl. Add milk or cream until the glaze is about the consistency of whipping cream. Drizzle over the cooled scones.

MAKES 8 SCONES

meyer lemon rolls

DOUGH

1 cup (250 mL) milk

⅔ cup (160 mL) sugar

1 tablespoon (15 mL) active
   dry yeast

5 cups (1.25 L) flour

½ cup (125 mL) butter,
   softened

zest of 1 Meyer lemon

½ teaspoon (2.5 mL) salt

2 eggs, lightly whisked

1 tablespoon (15 mL)
   vegetable oil

FILLING

1 cup (250 mL) sugar

½ teaspoon (2.5 mL) salt

zest of 1 Meyer lemon

2 tablespoons (30 mL) Meyer
   lemon juice

¼ cup (60 mL) butter,
   softened

GLAZE

2 cups (500 mL) icing sugar

zest of 1 Meyer lemon

2 tablespoons (30 mL) Meyer
   lemon juice

pinch salt

whipping cream to thin

The slight sweetness of Meyer lemons makes for a soft, well-rounded breakfast roll that is essentially a cinnamon bun without the spice. I use zest in all three parts of the recipe to give lots of flavour, but it's the glaze drizzled over at the end that really caps it all off. You'll need three Meyer lemons for the whole recipe.

In a small saucepan, warm the milk until it reaches about 100°F (40°C). Add to the bowl of a stand mixer fitted with the paddle attachment, then add a pinch of the sugar and sprinkle the yeast over the milk. Stir lightly and let sit until foamy, about 5 minutes.

Add the rest of the sugar, 3 cups (750 mL) of flour, and the butter, lemon zest and salt. Mix on low speed until well combined, about 2 or 3 minutes. Add the rest of the flour and pour the whisked eggs over the dough. Switch to the dough hook and knead the dough on medium speed until smooth and elastic, but still slightly sticky, about 5 to 7 minutes.

Add the vegetable oil to a large bowl and, using your fingertips, brush it up the side of the bowl. With your oiled fingers, transfer the dough to the bowl and turn to coat. Cover the bowl with plastic wrap and set aside somewhere warm until the dough has doubled in size, about 1 to 1½ hours.

While the dough is rising, prepare the filling. In a small bowl, combine the sugar, salt and zest. Mix with your fingertips until the zest is worked into the sugar and the sugar is pale orange in colour and has a sandy texture. Sprinkle the lemon juice over and mix again until it forms a sort of paste.

Butter two 9-inch (23 cm) cake pans or pie plates.

When the dough has doubled in size, divide in half. Sprinkle the counter with a bit of flour and shape the dough into a rough rectangle. Roll out the dough into a large rectangle, about 12 × 16 inches (30 × 40 cm) and ¼ inch (6 mm) thick. Using a butter knife or offset spatula, spread 2 tablespoons (30 mL) of the butter all over the dough. Sprinkle half of the sugar-lemon mixture over the dough and spread evenly, pressing into the dough slightly.

RECIPE CONTINUED ON NEXT PAGE

Starting with the long edge, roll the dough into a log, keeping it as tight as possible. Pinch the seam shut. Slice the log evenly into thirds and then each third into 3 or 4 pieces (depending on if you want 9 large rolls or 12 smaller ones). Repeat with the second half of the dough.

Place the sliced rolls cut side up in the prepared pan, spacing them evenly. (For 9 rolls, place 1 in the middle and 8 around it; for 12 rolls, centre 3 in the middle of the pan, with some space between, and place the remaining rolls around them.) Cover and let rise until doubled, about 1 hour.

Preheat the oven to 350°F (175°C). Bake the rolls until golden, about 27 to 35 minutes.

While they bake, make the glaze by mixing together the icing sugar, Meyer lemon zest and juice and salt in a bowl. Add cream to thin if it appears too thick.

Remove the rolls from the oven and let cool for 5 to 10 minutes before drizzling the glaze over them. Serve immediately.

MAKES 18 TO 24 ROLLS

pucker pull-apart loaf

DOUGH

½ cup plus 2 tablespoons (155 mL) milk

¼ cup (60 mL) sugar

2¼ teaspoons (11 mL) active dry yeast

2¾ cups (685 mL) flour

¼ cup (60 mL) butter

2 eggs, lightly beaten

½ teaspoon (2.5 mL) salt

1 tablespoon (15 mL) vegetable oil

FILLING

½ cup (125 mL) sugar

zest of 1 grapefruit

zest of 1 lemon

zest of 1 lime

¼ cup (60 mL) butter, melted

GLAZE

½ cup (125 mL) icing sugar (approximately)

1 teaspoon (5 mL) each grapefruit, lemon and lime juice

pinch salt

A few years ago, pull-apart loaves were popping up all over the food blog world. There were savoury varieties—think Buffalo chicken or garlic and herb—and sweet ones like cinnamon and sugar. And then, suddenly, there were lemon versions everywhere. Making one was always on my to-do list, but when I gave it more thought, I realized I wanted an all-citrus loaf—one that uses lemon, lime and grapefruit—to really add a lot of flavour. Perfect for brunch, this loaf is equally good on lazy weekend afternoons with a cup of coffee or tea.

In a small saucepan set on the stove, heat the milk until just warm to the touch.

In the bowl of a stand mixer fitted with the paddle attachment, combine a pinch of the sugar and the yeast. Pour the milk in and let bloom until foaming and creamy looking, about 5 minutes. Add the rest of the sugar and the flour, butter, eggs and salt. Mix on low speed until the dough starts coming together. Switch the paddle for the dough hook and knead the dough until it is smooth and shiny, about 5 minutes.

Add the oil to a large bowl and, using your fingertips, brush it up the side of the bowl. With your oiled fingertips, scoop the dough into the bowl, turning it to coat. Cover with plastic wrap and set aside somewhere warm to rise until dough has doubled in size, about 1 hour.

While it rises, mix the filling. In a small bowl, combine the sugar and citrus zests. Mix with your fingertips until it is sandy in texture.

Butter a 9- × 5-inch (23 × 12 cm) loaf pan that is 3 inches (8 cm) deep.

Roll the dough out into a rectangle about 20 × 12 inches (50 × 30 cm) in size. Spread the melted butter all over the dough and sprinkle with the sugar-zest mixture, pressing it lightly into the dough.

Cut the dough vertically into 5 strips about 4 inches (10 cm) wide. Stack the 5 strips of dough on top of each other, with all the sugared sides facing up. Cut them into 6, creating rectangles of about 4 × 2 inches (10 × 5 cm).

RECIPE CONTINUED ON NEXT PAGE

Add the dough pieces to the prepared loaf pan, standing them on edge, with all the sugared sides facing the same way. The dough edges should be facing up, like the pages of a book. Cover and let rise until the dough has risen again, between 30 and 60 minutes. As it rises, preheat the oven to 350°F (175°C).

Bake the loaf until golden brown and cooked through, about 30 to 35 minutes. Check on it at the 20-minute mark to ensure it's not browning too quickly. If the edges are getting dark, cover loosely with foil and continue baking.

While it bakes, make the glaze. Whisk together the icing sugar and grapefruit, lemon and lime juices, as well as the salt. Add more juice or sugar as necessary to get a consistency like that of whipping cream.

Let the loaf cool for 10 to 15 minutes and then drizzle with the glaze.

MAKES 1 LOAF

grapefruit-lemon marmalade

1 large grapefruit
3 large lemons
8 cups (2 L) water
8 cups (2 L) sugar

I was toying with the idea of writing a cookbook when I was invited to lunch with two of Canada's pre-eminent food writers, Elizabeth Baird and Rose Murray. They were on a tour for their latest cookbook, *Canada's Favourite Recipes*, so I told them about my plan to write one of my own, all about citrus. They encouraged me to make the pitch, and months later, when I told Baird my dream was coming true, she offered to share this recipe for marmalade. She notes that "White grapefruit will make a more golden marmalade; pink or red, a rosier spread. All are good."

Cut a 10-inch (25 cm) square of double-thickness fine cheesecloth and set aside.

Scrub grapefruit and lemons in warm, sudsy water. Trim off the blossom ends and any blemishes. Cut the fruit in half and squeeze out the juice, dislodging seeds. Strain the juice into a large saucepan, reserving seeds and any pulp. Pull the membranes out of the grapefruit and lemon halves, leaving just the rinds.

Place seeds, pulp and membranes in the centre of the prepared cheesecloth. Bring up the sides loosely, but so they're completely enclosing the contents, and tie the top with string. Add the bundle to the saucepan.

Cut the hollowed-out lemon rinds into quarters and grapefruit rinds into sixths or eighths. Stacking 4 pieces together at a time, cut crosswise into the thinnest possible slices. Add the slices to the saucepan and then add the water.

Bring to a simmer over medium heat. Simmer gently, uncovered, periodically pressing the bag to release pectin, until the peel is translucent and soft enough to mush between your fingers, about 2 hours. Measure the peel mixture; there should be 8 cups (2 L). If there is more, boil to reduce mixture; if less, add water to make up the difference. Divide the mixture in half.

For each batch, measure 4 cups (1 L) of the peel mixture and half of the sugar into a heavy-bottomed saucepan. Stir well and bring to a boil over high heat. Boil vigorously, stirring constantly, until marmalade clears, thickens and reaches setting point (see note), about 10 to 12 minutes.

Pour into clean, hot preserving jars, leaving a ¼-inch (6 mm) headspace. Seal with discs and bands. Boil on a rack in a covered boiling water canner, ensuring the boiling water covers the jars by at least 2 inches (5 cm), for 10 minutes. Uncover the canner and let the boiling subside. Remove the jars and let cool on a folded towel or on racks for 24 hours. Check that the jar lids have snapped down. Refrigerate any jars whose lids have not and consume the contents within 3 weeks. The rest can be stored in a cool, dark place, for up to a year.

MAKES ABOUT EIGHT 1-CUP (250 ML) JARS

To test for setting point, place 2 small plates in the freezer an hour before boiling the fruit and sugar. As the marmalade mixture boils, its foamy bubbles clear and increase in size, breaking noisily. The juices start to thicken. About 5 minutes before the suggested boiling time above, take the marmalade off the heat. Dribble about a ½ teaspoon (2.5 mL) of the marmalade onto 1 of the plates. Let it cool, about 1 minute. Run the tip of a spoon through the marmalade; if the surface of the marmalade wrinkles, the marmalade is ready to jar. If the blob of marmalade does not wrinkle, return the pan to the heat and the plate to the freezer. Stirring constantly, continue boiling, and test every 3 or 4 minutes until the setting point is reached. Always use the colder of the 2 plates, and always remove the saucepan from the heat while testing.

basics

citrus curds

lemon curd

zest and juice of 4 lemons
   (about 1 cup [250 mL])
   (see note)
1 cup (250 mL) sugar
3 eggs
1 egg yolk
½ cup (125 mL) butter, cut
   into cubes
½ teaspoon (2.5 mL) salt

Soft and rich, tart and tangy, citrus curds have a multitude of uses. One friend stirs it into her yogurt; my mum prefers to dip homemade shortbread in to eat, while others I know spread it on toast or simply eat it straight from the container with a spoon. More traditionally—and historically—it's served with scones as part of an afternoon tea. Here are three versions to try: Lemon, Lime (see note) and Meyer Lemon.

In a double boiler or a metal bowl set over a pot of simmering water, whisk together the zest, juice, sugar, eggs and egg yolk. Whisk constantly until the mixture thickens and reaches 160°F (71°C) on a thermometer. Turn off the heat and add the butter a few cubes at a time, whisking them in and waiting for them to disappear before adding more. Stir in the salt.

Strain the curd through a fine-mesh sieve into a bowl. Cover with a piece of plastic wrap, pressing it right onto the curd to prevent a skin from forming. Let cool to room temperature and then refrigerate.

MAKES ABOUT 2½ CUPS (625 ML)

RECIPE CONTINUED ON NEXT PAGE

To make Lime Curd, simply substitute the zest of 5 limes and 1 cup (250 mL) juice in place of the lemon. Follow the rest of the instructions as above.

meyer lemon curd

1 tablespoon (15 mL) Meyer
   lemon zest
½ cup (125 mL) Meyer lemon
   juice
½ cup (125 mL) sugar
2 eggs
2 egg yolks
¼ cup (60 mL) butter, cubed
¼ teaspoon (1 mL) salt

In a double boiler or a metal bowl set over a pot of simmering water, whisk together the zest, juice, sugar, eggs and yolks. Whisk constantly until the mixture thickens and reaches 160°F (71°C) on a thermometer. Turn off the heat and add the butter a few cubes at a time, whisking them in and waiting for them to disappear before adding more. Stir in the salt.

Strain the curd through a fine-mesh sieve into a bowl. Cover with a piece of plastic wrap, pressing it right onto the curd to prevent a skin from forming. Let cool to room temperature and then refrigerate.

MAKES ABOUT 1½ CUPS (375 ML)

lemon-honey butter

½ cup (125 mL) butter,
  softened
2 tablespoons (30 mL) honey
zest of 1 lemon
1 tablespoon (15 mL) lemon
  juice
pinch flaked sea salt or fleur
  de sel

Sweet, tart, with a hint of salt, this compound butter hits a lot of notes. Lovely on toast, it's even better on fresh-baked scones or biscuits, especially when still warm from the oven. Although this version calls for lemon, using Meyer lemons or limes is a nice way to switch things up.

In a small bowl, combine the butter, honey, lemon zest and juice and salt. Stir well to combine, then cover (or scrape into a jar or container with a lid) and refrigerate.

MAKES ½ CUP (125 ML) BUTTER

meyer lemon dressing

2 tablespoons (30 ml) Meyer
  lemon juice
1 teaspoon (5 mL) honey
⅛ teaspoon (0.5 mL) salt
freshly ground pepper
3 tablespoons (45 mL)
  vegetable or canola oil

The light taste of Meyers makes for a milder dressing that's ideal for simple green salads. This version is very basic because I didn't want stronger flavours to mask the fragrant lemon juice.

In a jar or container with a lid, combine the Meyer lemon juice, honey, salt and pepper. Give it a few shakes to dissolve the salt and honey, then add the oil. Shake again until emulsified.

MAKES ABOUT ¼ CUP (60 ML) DRESSING

lemon-infused olive oil

peel of 2 lemons
1 cup (250 mL) extra virgin
  olive oil

Use this infused oil for salad dressings, for drizzling over the Baked Ricotta with Lemon and Chives (page 33) or anywhere else that calls for oil where a little bit of lemon flavour would be a welcome addition. This will work with either Meyer lemons or regular ones. Easily double or triple the recipe to have extra on hand, if desired.

Scrub the lemons well and then remove the peels with a vegetable peeler or sharp knife, taking care to avoid the bitter pith. In a small saucepan or pan set over low heat, warm the olive oil and lemon peels for about 20 minutes. Let cool and strain out the peels. Pour the oil into a jar or bottle and seal. Store in the fridge.

MAKES 1 CUP (250 ML)

lemon aioli

1 egg yolk

1 clove garlic, grated

1 teaspoon (5 mL) lemon zest

1 teaspoon (5 mL) Dijon
mustard

salt

1 cup (250 mL) neutral oil, like
canola (see note)

2 tablespoons (30 mL) lemon
juice, divided

Until only a few years ago, mayonnaise was one of those things I refused to eat. I've started to come around, though I still rarely eat it without mixing in some herbs, spices or citrus. Recently, I started to make my own. Although I often hear horror stories about aiolis breaking, the method of adding only a spoonful of oil at a time while whisking has made this virtually foolproof. This is a solid, lemon-tinged basic aioli. Dress it up with herbs or more garlic or lemon zest for even more flavour.

Roll up a towel and form into a circle. Place a large bowl in the centre; the towel will keep it from moving around the counter while you're whisking.

Add the yolk, garlic, lemon zest, mustard and a pinch of salt to the bowl and whisk until mixed. Add the oil one spoonful at a time, whisking constantly, waiting until each is completely mixed in before adding the next one.

Once half the oil has been whisked in, add half the lemon juice and whisk until completely incorporated. At this point, the oil can be added in a slow drizzle while constantly whisking or you can continue adding it a spoonful at a time, if desired.

After you've added all the oil, lightly whisk the remaining lemon juice into the aioli and add salt to taste, about ¼ teaspoon (1 mL).

MAKES ABOUT 1 CUP (250 ML)

Don't bother with extra virgin olive oil, which will make the aioli far too bitter. I prefer canola oil or vegetable oil, which are neutral enough that they don't overpower the lemon.

preserved lemons

⅓ to ½ cup (80 to 125 mL)
  coarse kosher salt
6 to 8 lemons, washed
  thoroughly
juice of 1 to 2 lemons, plus
  more if neded

Regular lemons and their oh-so-fragrant cousins, Meyer lemons, work equally well, though they will have slightly different flavours, in the end. The only real trick to this recipe is patience and planning, as it will take a few weeks for the lemons to be fully preserved. For a faster version, try Quick Preserved Lemons (page 201).

Sterilize a 4-cup (1 L) canning jar. In the bottom of the jar, sprinkle a couple of tablespoons of the salt.

Cut about ¼ inch (6 mm) off the stem end of each lemon and then slice lengthwise in quarters, but keeping the base intact, so the 4 pieces are still attached at the bottom. Pack the centre of the lemon with salt and then add it to the jar. Repeat with each of the lemons, squishing them tightly as you pack them into the jar, releasing some of their juice. Once the jar is full, top up with additional lemon juice so the lemons are fully covered. Sprinkle with another couple of tablespoons of salt and seal the jar.

Let the jar of lemons sit at room temperature for 2 or 3 days, shaking the jar occasionally. Move it to the fridge and let the lemons cure for 3 weeks or longer.

To use a lemon, rinse it with cold water and remove any seeds, then proceed with the recipe that calls for it.

MAKES 6 TO 8 PRESERVED LEMONS

quick preserved lemons

2 lemons

1 tablespoon (15 mL) coarse
   salt

I will readily admit these are not authentic and would probably offend anyone making real Moroccan cuisine. But I think we can agree that we don't always have the time or—maybe more likely—the forethought to have preserved lemons on hand whenever we need them. Such was the case when I went to make my Moroccan Stew with Preserved Lemon (page 96) and realized that I was out. This is a down-and-dirty way to make them and they work beautifully in the stew.

Take 1 lemon and slice it into rounds about ¼ inch (6 mm) thick, reserving the very ends if there is any bit of fruit on them. Squeeze those ends and the juice of the remaining lemon into a measuring cup, adding cold water to make up a ½ cup (125 mL) of liquid in total.

Add the lemon slices, squeezed juice and salt to a small frying pan with a tight-fitting lid and set over high heat. Bring to a boil and stir to dissolve the salt, then reduce to medium-low and cover with the lid. Simmer the lemon slices for 10 to 20 minutes, until they are tender and the rinds have gone translucent. Take off the heat and remove the slices to a container to cool or use immediately. Discard the cooking liquid.

MAKES 1 PRESERVED LEMON

citrus-pickled onions

½ cup (125 mL) white vinegar
juice of 2 limes, strained
juice of 2 lemons, strained
⅓ cup (80 mL) sugar
5 whole cloves
5 whole peppercorns
¼ teaspoon (1 mL) mustard
  seeds
¼ teaspoon (1 mL) coriander
  seeds
¼ teaspoon (1 mL) salt
1 bay leaf
1 red onion, cut in half and
  thinly sliced

These onions turn a glorious shade of pink when pickled with lemon and lime and get great flavour from the spices. They're perfect on Citrus-Braised Pork Shoulder Tacos (page 104), but I love them equally in sandwiches or on pieces of toast covered in mashed avocado.

In a small saucepan set over medium-low heat, combine the vinegar, lemon and lime juices, sugar, spices, salt and bay leaf. Warm, stirring occasionally, until the sugar and salt have dissolved. Add the sliced onion to the saucepan and stir, cooking until they are softened and everything has turned bright pink, about a minute or two. Remove from the heat and let cool, then refrigerate.

These will keep in the fridge for a couple of weeks, if they last that long.

MAKES 2 CUPS (500 ML)

guacamole

2 avocados

½ teaspoon (2.5 mL) lime zest

2 tablespoons (30 mL) lime
juice

a few pinches of salt

½ jalapeño, seeded and finely
diced

¼ cup (60 mL) cilantro,
coarsely chopped

3 tablespoons (45 mL) finely
diced yellow onion

I used to make a guacamole full of tomatoes and garlic and other accoutrements, but then I tried a much simpler version and fell in love with the clean flavour. The fact that it requires much less chopping is just a bonus. Since I'm a spice wimp, I use only half a jalapeño. Those looking for more kick will want to use the entire pepper.

Cut the avocados in half, remove the pits and, taking care not to cut through the skins, slice horizontally and vertically to create small cubes. Use a spoon to scoop the flesh out into a bowl, then lightly mash about half of the avocado cubes. Add the lime zest, juice and salt to taste, and stir lightly. Add the jalapeño, cilantro and onion, then mix well. Cover with plastic wrap, pressing it down against the guacamole, and refrigerate for about 20 minutes.

MAKES ABOUT 2 CUPS (500 ML)

pico de gallo

4 Roma tomatoes, diced

½ jalapeño, seeded and finely
diced

½ cup (125 mL) finely diced
yellow onion

¼ cup (60 mL) cilantro,
coarsely chopped

2 tablespoons (30 mL) lime
juice

salt to taste

So much fresher than jarred salsa, this Pico de Gallo perks up tortilla chips and goes well with tacos. Since I like mine on the milder side, I've called for only half a jalapeño. Those who like it spicier will probably want to use the entire thing.

Add all the ingredients to a bowl, mix well and then cover with plastic wrap. Refrigerate for about 30 minutes before serving.

MAKES ABOUT 2 CUPS (500 ML)

ricotta

3 cups (750 mL) whole milk
(3.25%)

1 cup (250 mL) whipping
cream

½ teaspoon (2.5 mL) coarse
sea salt

3 tablespoons (45 mL) lemon
juice

Lemon is not a flavouring for this recipe, but the acidic juice is essential to making this cheese. Perfect on its own, it's also lovely when drizzled with a bit of olive oil. Serve with crackers or crusty bread, or use as the basis for Baked Ricotta with Lemon and Chives (page 33), Lemon Soufflé Pancakes (page 163) and Lemon-Ricotta Muffins (page 167).

In a large saucepan, mix together the milk, cream and salt. Heat until the mixture reaches 190°F (88°C), stirring every so often to keep it from burning. Remove from the heat and add the lemon juice. Stir, gently, once or twice and then let sit for 5 minutes so the curds and whey separate.

Line a large sieve or colander with 2 or 3 layers of cheesecloth and place over a bowl. Pour the mixture into the sieve and let it strain for at least an hour, or more, depending on how firm you like it. (I usually stop draining mine after an hour and a quarter.) It will firm up more once refrigerated.

Eat the ricotta immediately or put into an airtight container and refrigerate.

MAKES A LITTLE MORE THAN 1 CUP (250 ML)

acknowledgements

This book has been a labour of love, imagination, research and more rounds of dirty dishes than I ever thought I'd wash.

None of it would have been possible without the support of my family and friends, who served as recipe testers, cheerleaders, mood boosters and counsellors.

Thanks to those who ate all those batches of muffins and lemon bars when I was sure one more round would be the one that would perfect the recipe. Thanks to those who liked my photos on social media, encouraging me with comments about how excited they were to try out the recipes on their own. Thanks also to friends who did not complain about the sheer number of photos I was posting to social media.

The photos in this book would not have been possible without the help of Leah Hennel and Stuart Gradon, who offered equipment and expertise to help me create the most mouth-watering images I could.

I have to particularly thank Julie Van Rosendaal, who answered every strange or neurotic question as I put this book together and who handed over her grandmother's Baked Lemon Pudding Cake recipe, as well as Chef Liana Robberecht, Chef Michael Allemeier and Elizabeth Baird, who also shared their recipes with me.

A special citrus-tinged thank you must be given to Katherine O'Neill, who eagerly tested every main dish and most of the soups and salads, offering solid advice and her own culinary expertise to make sure each one was as good as it could be. Thank you, friend; the next bottle of wine is on me. I'll pick something that pairs well with citrus.

index